A WHIS LOAN IN
GOD'S EAR

A Whisper in God's Ear

Tom Acierno

Arbor Books, Inc.

For more information, please contact:
tom@tomacierno.com

Book design by:
Henry Conant
Arbor Books, Inc.
19 Spear Road, Suite 301
Ramsey, NJ 07446
www.arborbooks.com

Printed in Canada

A Whisper in God's Ear
Tom Acierno

1. Title 2. Author 3. Religion & Spirituality

LCCN: 2008927174

ISBN 10: 0-9800582-7-9
ISBN 13: 978-0-9800582-7-7

TABLE OF CONTENTS

This book is dedicated to the loving memories of
Florence "Monee" Acierno
Felix R. Acierno, Sr.
William H. "Bud" Holmes
Lorraine Burgett Holmes
Terry O'Connor
Robert B. Seybold
And all of those who have walked this Earth
with grace and dignity

I'm not sure what they would think about this book, but
I'll ask the next time I see them.

ACKNOWLEDGEMENTS

I wish to thank my family and friends who have supported me and encouraged me to follow my heart and publish this book.

I am deeply and most sincerely grateful to Larry Leichman, Joel Hochman, Steven DeRosa, Chris Hammer, Susan Lago, Kelly Epperson, Christopher Cella, Jessica Gorham, Michael Lorbeer, Elise Vaz and all of the wonderful folks at Arbor Books who have made the publication of this book a reality.

FOREWORD

Centuries ago, people fervently believed that the Earth was flat. It was common knowledge, an accepted fact. If we sailed too far, we would fall off the edge, and be consumed by dragons and monsters. This was not just the thinking of an average uneducated person; the supposedly intelligent people also believed this worldview. People thought that the Earth was flat because they did not have the facts or the perspective to support what we know today.

Spiritually speaking, many of us are still on that flat world, simply accepting what we are told by others to be the true and correct facts. We are using a two-thousand-year-old book with questionable translations as our moral compass. From a spiritual standpoint, in our guidebook, the Earth is still flat, and most people are still afraid to sail toward the edge.

It is a far different world today than it was two thousand years ago. Man's knowledge, and hopefully his wisdom, have expanded. Man's understanding of his world and his relationship with God has evolved.

We no longer ceremoniously slit the throats of unblemished lambs to let them bleed out at the altar, in appeasement to God. Nor do we tell every person born blind that the reason they are blind is because God has cursed them. We do not stone people to death for perceived acts of religious disobedience.

It takes courage to challenge traditional, accepted religious teachings, and I would like to thank all who have had the daring to question what they have been taught. It is not a matter of disrespect, heresy or sacrilege. In fact, it is just the opposite. Every individual needs to examine his own belief system to understand fully why he believes what he claims to believe. It is the most spiritual action a person can take. I believe that God welcomes our questions and our desire to understand his love more fully.

Religion and spirituality are topics that inspire faith and charity, passion and compassion. Unfortunately, they also inspire hatred, prejudice and bigotry. It is amazing and sad that something that is supposed to be founded on a profound sense of love, mercy and grace can also become so misguided as to breed and fuel violence, hypocrisy, closed minds and the divisiveness of humanity.

Of one thing I am sure: God is a god of love, and he weeps with a broken heart when he sees his children acting out in terrible ways and proclaiming that their actions are done "in the name of God." Regardless of our color, creed, race or religion, we are all children of God. To honor God is to love our fellow men, no matter what belief, or nonbelief, they hold.

For those of you who have given God and spiritual matters serious reflection and have come away content and satisfied within your religious beliefs, I commend you. For those of you who feel that there is more to spirituality than merely sitting in a house of worship once a week, read on. Your spiritual awakening is about to begin.

I am not a religious scholar, nor do I profess to be one. I'm a regular working stiff, your average Joe. I'm any Tom, Dick or Harry you went to school with or worked with over the years. In fact, my name is Tom. Just like many of you, I'm among the Baby Boomer generation; I've raised a family and am still working, hoping for a decent retirement. I've had the same ups and downs in life as most other folks, and for most of my life, I've accepted that there was a God, but never really gave him or religion much thought.

My attitude was similar to our ancestors, who believed the Earth was flat. I was raised Catholic, and even in my adult life, on most Sundays, you could find me sitting in a church pew. I enjoyed attending mass and it was a part of my weekly routine. Going to church was expected and accepted, and just like breathing, I didn't think about it. I believed whatever the church told me about God. I never questioned anything or gave any issue a second thought.

My true spiritual quest did not begin until 1991,

after certain events in my life got me thinking, for the first time, about what really happens to our souls, and the ultimate existential question of our earthly lives: What's it all about?

Call it a nudge from God, call it whatever you want; I was driven to research what life, death and spirituality truly are, and to put the results of that research on paper. This book represents my personal story of discovery. Whether or not these thoughts have been inspired or influenced by someone higher than myself is for you to decide. I have already made up my own mind.

This book is not fiction. It is spiritual reality, as I understand it to be. All I ask is that you read this book with an open mind. I do not want you to just accept what is written on these pages. I want you to read slowly and really think about what you are reading. Make up your own mind, draw your own conclusions, do your own research and embark on your own spiritual quest. My goal and purpose is not to convince anyone that I have all the answers. I feel at peace with my searching and what I have come to believe. I want you to know that same peace. But you have to make the voyage of discovery for yourself.

Spirituality is not only about people gathering to embrace and worship God; it is also about our personal and private journey toward God. No one else can nor should try to make that passage for you. It is an intimately personal journey and the most important journey you will ever make.

If you are someone who likes to think for yourself, if you are someone who would like to exercise the free will given to you by God, read on and open your mind to the timeless beauty of God's love.

The journey will not disappoint you!

CHAPTER 1

THE JOURNEY BEGINS

1

> *"Never lose an opportunity of seeing anything*
> *beautiful, for beauty is God's handwriting."*
> —*Ralph Waldo Emerson*

Sitting at her bedside, I stroked her hair. My mother was calm, yet her eyes beseeched me. My siblings and I knew that this hospital bed was indeed the deathbed, and that these hours would be her last moments with us here on Earth. It was an honor to spend that time with my mother, comforting her, as she so often had comforted me throughout my growing up. I was a grown man now, with a family of my own, and I thanked Mom for all she had done for us. My mother had been a positive influence on my life, and now I felt privileged to be a positive influence at her death.

I held her hand, I tenderly rubbed lotion on her feet, and I wiped her brow. I fluffed the sterile pillows and adjusted her blankets. I gave her ice chips and felt delighted when she smiled, as I knew her smiles were rapidly fading. She was lucid and asked me to tell her what I had learned on my journey, my spiritual journey. Gladly, I shared with her. My words brought her peace and I am forever grateful for that. She slipped into a comatose state and we knew her time with us was short. I was so moved and relieved that I could share with her what I had learned.

Being witness to her passing from this life into the next has impacted me forever. I was at her bedside and through her cracked lips and parched mouth, my mother began to speak. She was not speaking English and she was not talking to me. She was speaking in tongues, and I knew she was conversing with the spirit world. My mother had never spoken in tongues in her entire life, and now she was speaking so rapidly, so excitedly. As fast as the thoughts flow from the brain, her words came that quickly.

She was barely alive, yet she was communicating with someone in the spiritual world. Her voice, now barely audible, was serene. That was the last time I heard my mother's voice. She was gone within hours—gone from me in this physical life, but not gone from existence. I know she is in the spiritual world, and I know she will return to the physical world. What I saw on her deathbed confirmed my beliefs.

What I shared with my mother, my spiritual journey,

I want to share with you. The words that gave her peace, I hope will do the same for you as well.

We are all on a spiritual quest, yet most of us are not aware of it. Life is so busy and, for many of us, life can be so stressful that it's all we can do to get through each day. We arise each morning, go through our grooming and coffee rituals, and then embark upon the daily routine. The next morning, we get up and do it all again. We do not have the time or the energy to think about God, life, religion, immortality or anything of a spiritual nature. All of our efforts are spent taking care of the mundane demands of work, family, food and shelter. Maybe we make time in the evening for *American Idol*, but thoughtful reflection on serious matters? Hand me the remote. I'm tired and I don't want to think.

Sound familiar? That was me too, for a lot of years. Well, I don't watch reality television shows, but you get my point. The daily grind really was a monotonous grinding on my soul. For most of us, life is all hustle and bustle. We wear our "busyness" like a badge of honor. Lying in a field of clover watching the clouds float by, pondering the grand scheme of things or contemplating the "big picture" is something that will have to wait until retirement. "What's it all about?" is not a question we stop and think about. Life is so hectic that if we ever have a spare moment, "life" is exactly what we don't want to think about.

But is it really just for the moment that we live? I don't think so. I believe that we live for eternity.

Most people and most religions believe in eternity and have some kind of theory of the afterlife. I held the traditional Christian viewpoint for most of my life. But something was missing. All the pieces of the puzzle did not add up for me. I did what many of us never allow ourselves to do: I started thinking and questioning and seeking answers. My journey was quite surprising. Now that I have achieved peace and confidence, I feel compelled to share the next phase of my journey with you.

The lifetime you are in, right now, is yours to live to the fullest. It is true that the daily demands of everyday life won't simply disappear just because you begin a spiritual expedition, but I promise you that once you open your eyes, and open your mind, you will enjoy life more fully. You will see more beauty. You will feel more peace. You will experience God's love more than you ever thought possible.

The old saying "take time to stop and smell the roses" is overused and underappreciated. We all need to take time to stop and smell the roses, the lilacs and the lilies of the valley. We need to fully employ all of our senses. Smell, sight, sound, touch and taste—soak it all up. Walk barefoot. Eat your meals slowly and savor the sensations on your taste buds. Look at the trees blooming with spring buds, or perhaps they are snow-covered. Notice their ever-changing beauty. Be aware of your surroundings. As you commute to work or drive to the grocery store, pretend it is the first time you have ever taken this route, and pay attention to what you see. You may be astounded.

Now, take a deep breath and feel your lungs expand. Shake your arms. Wiggle your body. Get the kinks out of your neck. You are about to take off on an important trek, so you should stand up and give yourself a good stretch. The most important muscle to loosen up is your mind. That is often the most difficult part. We have thought patterns ingrained in our psyches that we are not even aware of. The sky is blue, the grass is green. The sun rises in the east and sets in the west. Our attitude about God is the same. It is something we accept as cold, hard truth without ever thinking twice about.

Maybe for you, God is a god of love, the Great Comforter. Perhaps you were raised to believe that God is a Judge and a Punisher. I once knew a man who said, "Going to church is supposed to be painful." For him, God was a god of wrath. For others, God is one more item on the to-do list. Go to church, say my prayers, make a confession; check, check, check. Many people go through the motions and their brains aren't in gear at all. God wants your heart, your soul and your mind. He wants you to be fully engaged.

We are surrounded by various religions, spiritual leaders and celebrities, all telling us what to think, what to believe. Television shows, seminars and radio programs are available and ready to "give you all the answers." God does not want us to take somebody else's word for it, to be spoon-fed.

You could close the book right now, because I am not one of those "experts" who's going to illuminate the path for you. My rationale is just the opposite. What God wants is for us to seek him ourselves. No one—not me, not Oprah, not the mystic at the top of the mountain—can satisfy your soul's longing for answers. That is between you and God. Certainly, many people can help you along your way, and I hope that I am one of them. I am simply here to tell you to "go for it," and I am one hundred percent confident that you will not be disappointed.

There has been a lot of talk in recent years about the purpose of life. I believe humans have wondered about that issue since the beginning of time. The purpose of life is to actively engage our minds, bodies and spirits to find God on our own, and to continually grow in compassion and knowledge. That discovery may or may not be within the realm of organized religion.

To start at the beginning, I believe God is the creator of Earth and man and all things. If you do not believe that, I will not try to persuade you. I am simply stating the groundwork for the beginning of my thought process. I believe God created me and gave me the gift of a free-thinking mind. We are not automated robots, set on autopilot, programmed to worship God. We must arrive at our conclusions about God on our own. That is how God wants it. My purpose for writing is to explain my path and hopefully propel you onto your own path.

We travel alone and we travel together, but each experience is interpreted by us individually. Humans are amazing creatures. We all have heard how several people can witness the same accident and all will tell different versions, describing it through their own unique perspectives. A group of friends can all take a walk together through the woods. One person will smell the heady scent of fragrant pine trees; one will see deer tracks faintly visible in the dirt; and one will hear the hushed sounds of a far-off babbling brook. We all focus differently. It is not my intent to guide your focus my way. My goal is for you to simply start to focus on your spirituality in your own way.

As we go through life, we all have moments of questioning and moments of appreciation. Religious or not, most of us have muttered a "please, God" or a "thank God." We have moment after moment of realization, but those moments come and go without fully registering in our hearts or in our minds. For some people, it takes a cataclysmic event to trigger a true soul-searching journey for God and for the meaning of our existence. For others, it is an accumulation of wondering over time that begins to culminate into a conscious desire to search for God, and to find some answers to the questions that nag at us.

What is it for you? Why are you holding this book? I do not mean this to be a trick question. There must have been something that led you to this moment, one in which this book piqued your curiosity. Last year or even last week, you may have glanced at the cover and passed it by without a second glance. Today, you are prompted to pick it up and leaf through the table of contents and flip through the chapters.

Maybe you had a death in the family and you are thinking about the ever after. Maybe you have reached a certain age and are beginning to contemplate your own mortality. Maybe you have no idea why, but you feel compelled to do a little digging and find out more about God and what he means for your life.

Whatever the reason, you are now in the frame of mind to think about God in new ways, or evaluate your current beliefs and reaffirm your old ways. The point, the glorious point, is that you are ready to focus on God. You are launching on a flight that will change your life, and improve your life. I am delighted and I am certain that God is, too. By embarking on a journey of discovery, you will be amazed at what happens when you engage your spirituality each and every day.

God is real and God wants us to seek him. Some find him in man-made religion, some don't. I left the familiarity of my church pew and Sunday morning traditions and actively started looking for God. I found him. You can, too.

CHAPTER 2

I EXIST BECAUSE...?

2

"I cannot tell the truth about anything unless I confess being a student, growing and learning something new every day. The more I learn, the clearer the view of the world becomes."
—*Sonia Sanchez*

Why do I exist? Why do you exist? Why do humans exist? Have you ever let this thought play around in your head? Questions concerning our very existence are hard to fathom and can be a little scary. We cannot comprehend all the mysteries of the universe, and the biggest mystery of all is staring back at us in the mirror.

Wondering

At birth, our metamorphic journey of life begins. For each of us, this lifetime will become the human adventure that leaves a lasting imprint on our souls. The escapade that we call physical life will humble some, inspire others and bring some to the brink of despair. Life can seem a tedious exercise that finds us scratching our heads, wondering what it is all about. Over the course of a lifetime of work and distraction, we all lose a little bit of ourselves. It is a slow, barely noticeable erosion of who we are. It seems unavoidable that each of us, at some point in our lives, will ask: Is this all there is?

Why do you believe that you are here on this Earth? Some of you may have considered this query earlier in your life; for others, it is not something you like to think about. I kindly ask that you give it a try. At least once in our lives we should ponder this difficulty, and I say that there is no better time than the present. Before you read further in this book, give the question some serious thought. Why are you here? Do you think you have a purpose?

Grab a piece of paper. Take a deep breath and relax. This is not a pop quiz, and no one will see your answers. There are no right or wrong responses. You won't get a red "X" or a gold star. This is only for you. Close your eyes. Listen to your breath go in and out. Put your hand on your chest and feel your heart beat. Keep your eyes closed; let your body relax and your mind unwind. Take your time. Our very existence is something that can be quite difficult to wrap our minds around, so don't worry if you feel slightly overwhelmed. Let the thought dance. Why am I here? What is my purpose in life? Do I even have a purpose in life?

Jot down whatever pops into your head. Don't write what you think you are "supposed to" write. This is a reflective assignment for you alone, and no one else needs to see your thoughts unless you want them to. Maybe you will want to keep this paper for future reflection and reference as you take off on your quest for God.

"Why am I here?" may be one of life's deepest questions. To help us sort through our thoughts, and whatever musings you wrote down, let's consider these probing points.

A) Are you satisfied with your life so far?
B) If not, what have you done about it? What can you do about it?
C) Do you think you will be able to fulfill or complete your purpose in your lifetime?
D) Do you feel that your life is on the right track?

Did you define a purpose for your life? Maybe you did not write down anything at all; that is fine. The point of the inquiry was to start you thinking. The whole point of this book is to prompt you to begin thinking on a spiritual level.

Perhaps you feel at peace. Maybe you sometimes feel helpless, as if you are floundering around in a world that seems out of control. When we read the newspaper and watch television, it often seems as if there is more bad than good going on in the world, but that is not the case. Our world is a divine combination of planned events and random occurrences. Does that sound confusing? Good. That means you are starting to mull over the complexity of life. By the time you finish this book, you'll see that the complex boils down to a few simple truths.

What Is It All About?

For now, let's not rush. Good things come to those who wait. The goal is to take time out from the crazy, roller-coaster, nonstop merry-go-round of everyday life; let yourself ruminate about life in general, and your life in particular. Do you like how it is going so far? If not, I think I can help you get on the right track. As you know, there is so much more to life than watching TV and paying the bills. I have figured out why I exist, and I want to help you figure it out, too.

When life's confusion makes our heads spin, that is exactly the time we need to concentrate on the part of our existence that can be the hardest to appreciate. We need to regain our spiritual compass. It requires a conscious commitment to seek spiritual calm, but I can testify that it is worth it.

Life here on Earth can be considered a spiritual training ground. Are you ready for basic training? Are you ready to find your place in God's universe? You won't need any special uniform, equipment or combat boots. This training can take place in the comfort of your favorite chair in front of the fireplace, or in a sailboat in the middle of the lake. As certain places make our spirits soar, so can finding God in our everyday life. Don't you want that wondrous feeling regularly?

What your grade-school teacher told you still rings true: We should learn something new every day. No one book or no one person should deliver enlightenment to you on a silver platter. Life is not one-size-fits-all, and it is not one heaping serving of knowledge, everything you need to know tied up in a pretty package. A journey requires that we discover things for ourselves; it is not a quick trip through a convenience store with one-stop shopping.

We should not go through life as a shadow, settling for only a fraction of what we could become on the spiritual, and human, level. It is not just the Army that wants you to "be all you can be." God wants that for you also. This life is indeed a gift not to be squandered.

Every life has divine purpose and meaning.

Seek and You Will Find

The first revelation I had as I started on this exploration was that questioning is not wrong. As parents, we encourage our children to be curious and seek answers for themselves. When a child figures out something for himself, the results are more meaningful and tangible. God is the ultimate example of a loving parent, and he is gratified that we care enough to want to know more about him and about ourselves. God has nothing to hide; in fact, he can't wait to reveal his truths. We just have to endeavor to investigate. There is an ancient proverb that states, "Truth fears no trial." It is not a sign of a lack of faith, or a sin, or a "bad thing" in any way, to ask God questions. God welcomes your questions, so please lose any apprehension about this right now. You will not be struck by lightning, and a plague of locusts will not come devour your garden if you pose a few questions to God. What will happen is the opposite. You will feel enveloped in a warm and loving embrace.

Once we get used to the idea that we can have doubts, and that it is okay to say, "Not everything I have believed my whole life makes sense to me," we need to realize that each individual learns in his or her own way, and in his or her own time. My research was primarily reading, analyzing, contemplating, praying and meditating on what I read. Nothing earth-shattering or avant-garde; it was simply a good, old-fashioned hunt for a remedy to soothe my searching soul. Not knowing can be the hardest thing in life; knowing provides the greatest blessing and peace of mind. You need to do your research your way. Reading this book is an excellent first step.

The second conclusion I reached is that each day offers an opportunity to grow in compassion and empathy toward others, and it is a responsibility to nurture our family and friends. Yet, we spend far too much time regretting past mistakes or worrying about a future still unknown. The here and now gets lost in the shuffle.

Bumper stickers and beer commercials may tell us to live in the moment, and we nod in agreement, but we seldom allow ourselves to do just that. However, living in the moment is essential to understanding what life is about. Here and now are the only certainties we have.

The more I read, studied and prayed, the clearer God spoke to me. No, I did not hear an audible voice. There was no burning bush or email memo from God. I describe it as an understanding washing over me. Pieces of the puzzle began to fall into place, and a feeling of confidence that I was on the right track permeated my being. The parts of the equation started to make sense.

Life does not have to be a riddle. Human beings have a difficult time accepting what the brain cannot comprehend or rationalize. For example, time has no beginning and no end. Space has no beginning and no end. The same can be said of knowledge. Time, space and knowledge go on forever. Forever is a tough concept to grasp. All we know, and all we need to know, is today.

Today I can show affection to my companion or spouse. Today I can be supportive of my children. Today I can be humble and accepting of my coworkers, my friends and those I encounter as I go about my day. Today I can pay attention to nature and the wonder of

God's creation all around me. Today I can be appreciative that I have this day to grow in compassion and in knowledge. Today I can grow closer to God.

What I learned, and what you will learn, too, is unmistakable. Looking for God is exactly what we are supposed to do.

CHAPTER 3

THE STORY OF MY DISCOVERY

3

"There are very few human beings who receive the truth, complete and staggering, by instant illumination. Most of them acquire it fragment by fragment on a small scale, by successive developments, cellularly, like a laborious mosaic."
—Anaïs Nin

Our modern mentality can often be expressed as, "I want it all and I want it now." We don't like to wait. We are a fast-food, fast-information culture. We want instant gratification. Knowledge does not work that way. It comes bit by bit, morsel by morsel and then chunk by chunk. Even great scholars of the Bible do not sit down and read the entire "Good Book" once through and declare, "Yes, now I know it all." Most things in life are a process, and accessing the spiritual level of living is no exception.

For some of us, we have completely fallen off our spiritual path and are wandering through life like a ship without a rudder. We turn this way and that, and have no bearings and no anchor. We may think, *Why bother with God?*, but whether we admit it or not, life is easier when we take care of all parts of our being: physical, mental, emotional and spiritual. We place so much emphasis on the physical, which is temporary, but the spiritual has ramifications that exceed the boundaries of what we can comprehend. The spiritual affects this life and all of eternity. Our spiritual side should not be ignored.

We avoid the spiritual facet because it is the hardest one to understand. Think about it from this perspective: If you give a two- or three-year-old child an Erector Set™, he may just sit there, stare at the pieces and not know what to do with it. Give this same set to a child of eight or nine years old, and he will build you an airplane, a skyscraper or a race car. We can use the same analogy with our spiritual life. God gives us so many gifts, so much to work with. Until we are ready, we just sit and stare and perhaps smack the pieces against each other. Then there comes a time when we see all the gifts before us, and understand that the magnitude of what we can do and what we can learn is limitless.

We are given gifts at different times, under different circumstances. Once you start to "tune in" to the spiritual, you will become aware of so much more around you. Spiritual growth can be exciting in the here and now, and ultimately, it enhances our soul for eternity. I feel that my own cosmic Erector Set™ has been given to me, and there is so much I can do with it. Maybe I was presented with the same set years ago and didn't know what to do. Everyone proceeds along the path at their own pace and we need to respect that. We also need to view all aspects or events of our lives, even the tragic ones, as opportunities to grow. Sometimes, that is easier said than done.

Not Really Looking for God

I plodded through my life like a lot of other people, not thinking about spiritual matters. Going to church on Sunday was routine. Thinking about God was not. Now, I think about my spirituality every day.

There was not a defining experience for me that switched on the ol' spiritual lightbulb. I did not have a dream and wake up shouting, "Eureka! I have found the meaning of life!" It has been a series of occasions that have made me pause, crinkle my brow and think, *Hmm*. Several incidents have individually and collectively caused the wheels of my mind to start turning.

Your desire to look for God may start out with a bang, and a pounding of the chest with wails of "why, God?" Your search for God may be more like mine: years of compiling questions until finally you decide to say, "Wait a minute. Just exactly what do I believe?" You may be a senior citizen, a Baby Boomer, a young mother or a teenage boy. The urge will strike and when it does, do not ignore it.

The Questions Begin

My wife, Phyllis, and I were very close to our parents, emotionally and logistically. Her folks, Lorraine and Buddy, lived just a few blocks from us. My father-in-law, at age eighty-two, suffered a massive coronary at home, and my wife arrived at their house as the paramedics worked on him. There would be no reviving him. Phyllis and her mother watched in awe as Buddy suddenly became alert. His eyes flew open wide and he looked at a point directly above them with such clarity that it was obvious to them that he was looking at someone or something. He was calm, unruffled, and then he was immediately pronounced dead.

Death is a common trigger for spiritual wondering. We hear many stories of people who have been with their loved ones as they departed this life. We've watched our comatose grandmothers break into joyful smiles as they flatline. We've seen our siblings whose bodies are racked with pain and disease slip away peacefully at the moment of passing. I witnessed my own mother speak in a language that she had never known or spoken as she left this physical world.

My father-in-law's death caused me to speculate on what he had been looking at. What did he see?

What happens when we die? Where do we go? I started reading books to help me find answers.

A week after Buddy's funeral, I let myself into my mother-in-law's place with my key. She called out to me from her bedroom, "Is he still here?" I had no idea what or whom she was talking about.

"There is no one here, Lorraine."

She informed me that a man had just been there, at the foot of her bed, and had walked out of the room when I came in. Before the words had left her mouth, I darted through the house, bolting from room to room, searching for an intruder. I went through the closets and looked in the shower and behind doors and curtains. The door had been locked when I came in. There was no sign of forced entry. I found no one in the house.

"Tom, don't panic. It's all right. He was only here to give me a message." My mother-in-law described in great detail a tall, kindly gentleman wearing a brown suit. He had walked into her room and had spoken to her. "Buddy sent me to tell you that he is okay and you should not worry. He is just fine."

Buddy and Lorraine were devout Catholics. They went to church every Sunday and were among the "good and faithful." My mother-in-law was one of the strongest people, mentally and spiritually, whom I had ever known. For Lorraine to say that she had seen a man with a message was very disconcerting. She was an honest, straightforward woman. She had a firm hold on her mental faculties and did not believe in ghosts.

I said nothing, but the look of doubt on my face must have been apparent.

"I am not crazy, Tom. It was not a dream. It was real. I know what I saw and I know what I heard. And you know that I am not one to make up stories."

That was true. My mother-in-law was the salt of the Earth. Her belief in seeing such a "vision" was as odd as if the Pope himself had claimed to see a herald from heaven. We trust certain people to be our rocks of faith, and it was out of character for Lorraine to speak of seeing this "spirit." Because it was so odd, and because it was her, it made me think that it had to be true. This woman was a credible witness; she was bright, trustworthy and still had all her wits about her. Her testimony would hold up in any court of law in any matter besides this, because of course, there is no way to prove a man appeared in her home and then vanished.

Lorraine didn't need proof. She believed. That is the essence of faith, perhaps. I believed her, too. If you knew her, you would as well. However, I understand that some people need a little more persuading. This "sighting" prompted me to read even more books.

Six months later, Lorraine was admitted to intensive care at a local hospital. Her health was failing fast, and this stalwart, Catholic pillar of the church was dying. My mother-in-law, a lifelong Christian, confided that she feared death. It didn't make sense to me that a woman who had spent every Sunday at mass should be afraid to meet her maker. She had no secrets or skeletons in her closet. How could a strong Christian be so afraid? She was one of the faithful, she held an unwavering belief throughout all the decades I had known her and yet, on her deathbed, she was not so sure. That stirred more questions in me.

The loss of Phyllis' parents within six months of each other created a difficult time for me. I also watched a coworker quietly suffer through the death of his little girl. It is hard enough to lose elderly parents, but to lose a child—that pain is unfathomable.

Then I was let go from my job. This created tremendous stress and turmoil for me. I had done nothing to deserve my pink slip. It was just the way of the corporate world. Downsizing was the buzz word of the decade, and I was among the many casualties.

With too much free time now as an unemployed, middle-aged guy, I watched the news channels and read the papers. There was so much "bad stuff" going on in the world. It was depressing. I started down the "what is life all about" trail of questions.

In my heart of hearts, I knew the world was not just doom and gloom. I knew there had to be answers. I knew I had to find mine. My spiritual quest now began in earnest.

Epiphany

Some find God while sitting in church. It certainly seems as if it should be the right place to find him. I was in church one Sunday morning, and I let my thoughts wander. I had planted myself in that pew for over fifty years. I liked going to church, the pageantry, the symbolism and the traditions. It dawned on me that going to church was like brushing my teeth, something I did without thinking, one more necessary part of a good, healthy and balanced life. The more I thought, the more I realized that I had been going through the motions. It seemed to me that there was something missing from my churchgoing. What was missing? My intimate connection to God.

So much of what I enjoyed about mass was simply the comfort and the familiarity. I started to analyze everything that I had believed my whole life. Before that moment, I had never thought it through, or thought about it at all. I chanted the words, I sang the hymns and I crossed myself, but I had never deliberated about the big picture. The symbolism now started to seem like a religious mask. I had been wearing a mask, too. I had merely shown up on Sundays and let someone else be in charge of what I thought and what I believed.

Realization hit me between the eyes: The whole point was supposed to be about me and God. God wants each of us to seek him out, and not just accept what we are told by those around us. We are to utilize our brains and our hearts in order to find out if God is real and what he wants for us.

After all those years of regularly attending mass, I had not yet found God in church, but it was in that place that I confronted my doubts and questions. In my neighborhood church, I discovered that I needed to find God.

Maybe I would find that he was in church all along, and maybe I wouldn't, but for the first time in my life, I was actively seeking God. I had to get off the church pew to do it. Perhaps, for some of you, you need to as well.

No offense or disrespect is intended. It is my mission to encourage, and my point is that many of us have been trapped in a repetitive habit. Take a look at your situation. Do you go to church because "it is the right thing to do" or because "it is what I have always done"? God wants you in church because you want to know him—no other reason.

And God is not just in church. He is everywhere. Do you want to find him? If you do, then get off your pew, get out of your recliner, get off your desk chair and turn off the computer and let's go find God.

CHAPTER 4

DEATH: IS IT REALLY THE GREAT UNKNOWN?

"*Dying is a very dull, dreary affair. And my advice to you is to have nothing whatever to do with it.*"
—W. Somerset Maugham

Let's face it. The only reason that we struggle with the questions of life, and tackle the perplexing puzzle of God, is because of the questions we have about death. Death is the dreaded conclusion, the great mystery, the feared unknown.

I have never known anyone to lie in bed at night worrying about ice cream. We know that if we run out of ice cream, we can go to the corner grocery store and buy more. Life does not work that way. We can't "buy more." We do not get an unlimited supply of hours and there is no fountain of youth that we can pull up to and say, "Fill 'er up."

Physical life does not go on forever, and at some point, each of us comes to the realization that our life is temporary. Living, as we know it, comes to an end, and that ending frightens some of us, and makes all of us wonder what does indeed happen when we take our last breath here on Earth.

"Contemplating death is the last thing I want to do." Have you ever heard anyone say that? It is an interesting play on words, because usually, if death does not come suddenly, contemplating death is in fact the last thing a person does.

It may appear that I have a morbid fascination with death; I do not. However, the subject of my mortality no longer bothers me or confounds me.

I believe with every fiber of my being that we never die. Each of us is eternal. Our physical body does not last indefinitely, that is true. But when physical death does occur, we don't drift off to the clouds, forever playing a harp in heaven, or burn in hell with a pitchfork in our hand, or wait for either of these two extremes in the limbo land called purgatory, as my Catholic upbringing taught me to believe.

I have no doubt. There is no death. There is so much more.

What Others Think

Along my sojourn, I researched other religions. Expanding my spiritual horizons did not necessarily mean that I wanted to convert to a different belief system, but I did feel the need to explore. In analyzing what I had always believed, it was helpful to learn about other religions and glean what I could from various backgrounds. Knowledge is always a worthwhile endeavor. Every culture, every religion must deal with physical death, and each does so in its own way.

The Hindu Perspective

At death, most Hindus are cremated. It is believed that cremation helps their souls escape more quickly from the body. In India, people hope to have their funeral at the burning *ghats* on the shores of the sacred River Ganges. At the holy river, the body is placed on a large pile of wood. The eldest son says the appropriate prayers and lights the fire. Incense is burned, and *ghee*, a type of clarified butter often used in sacrifice rituals, is poured onto the flames.

Now, this procedure may seem very strange to our Western sensibilities. We cannot imagine watching a ceremony of the body of our loved one being sent up in flames. It is eye-opening, and mind-opening, to learn of how others pay their respects.

After the funeral, the Hindu widow or widower wears white as a sign of mourning. The immediate family mourns for twelve days. On the thirteenth day, there is another ceremony, called Kriya, in which rice balls and milk are offered to the dead person to show the gratitude of the family for the life of that person.

After this, the mourners can continue on with their normal lives.

The Judaism Perspective

Followers of the Jewish faith hold an opposite perspective. Cremation is generally not customary, as it is seen as defiling the body, which is believed to be created in God's image. Death is understood as a natural part of the life cycle and the body is returned to the earth from whence it came.

Jewish tradition mandates burying the dead as soon as possible. The body is buried, usually in a linen cloth and in a simple pine box with no metal hardware, to promote quick decomposing. Embalming is a violation of Jewish tradition because it impedes the natural decomposition process. Dust to dust is wanted to occur expeditiously.

The casket remains closed. There is no visitation or viewing of the body. It is traditional to have people watch over the casket from the time of death until the burial, never permitting it to be alone. The watching over the body is done out of respect. Flowers, being temporary, are not brought to the funeral or to the mourners because they will only remind the family of their loss.

The immediate family will sit *shiva* for seven days. They do not leave the home for these seven days. Family and friends bring food to them. When people visit the grave, they may leave a small stone , signifying eternity. The stone lasts forever and so does the soul.

The Sikh Perspective

For the Sikhs, death is considered to be just one stage in the ongoing life of the soul. There is no mourning at a funeral for a Sikh since Sikhs believe that the soul never dies; it is progressing toward God. The body is usually washed by the family and new clothes are put on it. What is known as the "five Ks of Sikhism" are worn: *kirpan,* the Sikh knife or ceremonial dagger; *kara,* a steel bracelet; *kachera,* a special undergarment; *kanga,* a wooden comb; and *kesh,* long, uncut hair. Sikhs do not ever cut their hair.

The body is cremated as soon as possible and the ashes are released into the nearest river. Special prayers are recited during the brief funeral ceremony before the cremation. Sikhs believe that God judges each soul at the time of death. If deemed pure enough, the soul will be able to dwell with God. If not, the soul will be reincarnated.

The Baha'i Perspective

For those who are followers of the Baha'i faith, upon physical death, cremation is forbidden. The body is buried as quickly as possible, preferably within twenty-four hours; it is not embalmed unless required by law. The body is washed carefully and wrapped in a shroud. The cloth should be silk or cotton.

Interment takes place nearby, no more than a one-hour travel time from the city or town where the death occurred. A burial ring is placed on the finger of the deceased. The body is laid to rest in a coffin made of fine hardwood, not softwood or metal, and is to be buried with the feet pointed toward the Holy Land. One atypical fact I learned is that Baha'is are encouraged to leave a will and it should include their wishes to be buried according to the Baha'i laws of burial, which are unfamiliar to many.

The Islamic Perspective

Muslims also bury their dead as soon as possible after death, avoiding the need for embalming or otherwise disturbing the body. In preparation for burial, the family or other members of the community will wash and shroud the body, which will then be wrapped in sheets of clean, white cloth, called the *kafan*.

The deceased is then transported to the site of the funeral prayers. These prayers are commonly held outdoors, in a courtyard or public square, not inside the mosque. The community gathers, and the *imam*, the prayer leader, stands in front of the body, facing away from the worshippers.

While all members of the community attend the funeral prayers, only the men of the community accompany the body to the gravesite. The deceased is laid in the grave, without a coffin if that is permitted by local law, on his or her right side, facing Mecca. At the gravesite, it is discouraged for people to erect tombstones or elaborate markers or to put out flowers or other items on the grave. Rather, one should humbly remember Allah and his mercy, and pray for the person who has died.

Loved ones and relatives observe a three-day mourning period, which includes increased devotion, receiving visitors and condolences and avoiding decorative clothing and jewelry. Widows observe an extended mourning period, four months and ten days long. During this time, the widow is not to remarry, move from her home or wear decorative clothing or jewelry.

The Christian Perspective

I was raised Catholic and my worldview was Christian, including burial preparation and funeral procedures. Christians are accepting of embalming. Burial and cremation are both suitable options. Viewing the dead body prior to the funeral is customary. If the body has to wait a week before it is buried, Christians have no problem with that. They will send flowers to the funeral home or to the mourning family. It does not matter how long a widow mourns or what she wears.

There is no set mourning period or special cloth to wrap the body. The idea of the family washing the body of their deceased loved one may surprise the average Christian. Funerals are held in a church or at a funeral home. The casket can be made of any material.

Christians do not have rigid rules regarding the rites of funerals. The practices for the Christian do not follow a strict set of procedures or specific guidelines, except possibly for the prayers and services offered, depending on the various denominations.

What happens with the body upon physical death among differing cultures and religions fascinates me. Habits may vary widely, but in all faiths, traditions are adhered to and how we mourn follows prescribed boundaries. We do what we are taught and what we are used to, what we grew up with, because there is comfort in ritual.

The Buddhist Perspective

Upon death Buddhists may or may not be cremated depending upon the particular culture and acceptance in the world region where the deceased lived. In the West, Buddhist funerals are usually held at a funeral home or in the home of the deceased and will often include a eulogy, prayers and remembrances of the departed. A predominant theme is the reminder that life is fleeting. One's state of mind at death is very important. A negative state of mind at death will have a negative (after-death) effect. A positive state of mind at death will have a positive (after-death) effect. Practitioners in different parts of the world may follow the same basic principles, but funeral practices and rituals vary.

Curiosity Did Not Kill the Cat

Curiosity is a natural inquisitive behavior and we should not deny it. It is how we learn. In fact, being curious has led to many great and useful discoveries. I was intrigued by the diverse convictions and customs held by other religions.

I respect the Hindu faith. Nonetheless, the practice of burning a dead body in public is not a part of our way of life here in the United States. Most people would have a difficult time accepting such a ritual that is literally foreign to our way of thinking. That is exactly why it is helpful to think about these things. We have a cultural mind-set and automatically assume our way is the right way when the truth is, our way is simply only one way.

I don't think I could put my wife's body on a stack of burning logs, but that is how I was raised. If I lived in India, it would seem normal and expected. The fact that each religion has its own strikingly different customs, traditions and rules grabbed my interest. I had been set in my ways for so long that I never gave any thought to what anyone else believed, and honestly, I doubt I even cared at all what others believed. I was surrounded by people who believed what I did, and the notion that there were other ways of doing things never occurred to me.

I also wanted to ascertain what other religions believe regarding the soul when a person dies. People of all faiths agree that the body does not live eternally. The body is cremated or returned to the Earth. People may argue over what is "proper" disposal of the body, but there is no argument that the physical body has one use only.

The key to my search for God, however, has little to do with the physical aspect of death. The million-dollar question is, What happens to our essence, our soul?

Religions do not agree on what happens next.

One Life or Many?

Hindu Belief

Hinduism is the most radically different of all the religions mentioned above. Hindus believe that people do not live and die just once, but are able to be reborn a number of times before reaching their final end state. The idea that a soul can be reborn into this world to live a new life is called reincarnation; most people have some idea of the concept.

For the Hindu believer, the human soul is immortal and passes from body to body at death. The Hindu sacred text likens the process to casting off old clothes and putting on new ones. Hindus do not believe that man is sinful; he is just ignorant of his true nature. In fact, man's soul is actually that of God, and not until they realize this will Hindus be free from the cycle of being reborn. Freedom comes when they learn they are divine and belong to God.

Sikh Belief

In Sikhism, there is no heaven or hell. The afterlife in the spiritual realm means living with God for eternity. To achieve this salvation, a person must have a deep faith and a close relationship with God. Getting close to

God happens through meditation. A person's attachment to worldly ways and material possessions prevents him from gaining salvation and being able to dwell with God. The cycle of reincarnation and rebirth happens if a person does not devote himself to meditation and the pursuit of growing closer to God. God will judge that the soul is not ready to be able to dwell with him.

Jewish Belief

Judaism does believe in the afterlife, and the Hebrew words *Olam Ha-Ba* mean "the world to come," but Jewish sacred texts and literature have little to say about what happens after death. This may seem surprising to non-Jews, as Christianity, which has its foundation in Judaism, focuses on eternal life.

Although Judaism is much more focused on actions than beliefs, the belief in the eternal soul is fundamental. Heaven is where the soul experiences the greatest possible pleasure—the feeling of closeness to God. Jewish people believe in one life, one death and one eternal life for the soul.

Baha'i Belief

The Baha'i concept of life after death is deeply integrated into teachings about the nature of the soul and the purpose of this earthly life. The soul does not die; it endures everlastingly. When the human body dies, the soul is freed from the physical body and the surrounding physical world and begins its progress through the spiritual world. Under Baha'i belief, the soul is not reborn in a different body.

Baha'is understand the spiritual world to be a timeless and placeless extension of our own universe— and not some physically remote or removed place. Heaven is a state of nearness to God; hell is a state of remoteness from God. Each state follows as a natural consequence of individual efforts, or the lack thereof, to develop spiritually. Beyond this, the exact nature of the afterlife remains a mystery. Bahá'u'lláh writes, "The nature of the soul after death can never be described."

Islamic Belief

Muslims believe that death is a departure from the life of this world, but not the end of a person's existence. Rather, eternal life is to come, and they pray for God's mercy to be with the departed, in hopes that they may find peace and happiness in the life to come.

Islam teaches that each person is born with a pure soul, with no past life. The progress of the soul starts after the physical death, so the soul does not return to this world after the death of the body. Those souls in paradise are advancing to higher and higher stages in knowledge and perfection of faith. Hell is meant to purify the effects of bad deeds, and so make them fit for further advancement. Hell's punishment is, therefore, not everlasting. It is one stage in the progression of the soul.

Christian Belief

Standard Christian belief, though variations occur between Catholicism and Protestantism, and then among differing denominations within various Protestant congregations, is that we are born into this world, we die, and then we spend eternity with God in heaven or with Satan in hell. Catholics believe in an intermediary place called purgatory. Protestants do not.

In general, it can be safely stated that all Christians believe that we are physically born once. We live once. We die once. After we die, we spend eternity in a "place": heaven or hell. Followers of the Christian faith believe that the soul is eternal, with one physical life here on earth, and one eternal life spent elsewhere.

Some Christian faiths use the phrase "born again" to indicate that they are now Christian and will have eternal spiritual life. The basic tenets of the Christian faith, in an oversimplified nutshell, are: 1) Humans are born with original sin—nothing we do can erase that sin or make us worthy to be with God; 2) God sent his son, Jesus, to die as a sacrifice for man's sins; 3) Accepting Jesus as the Christ, the bridge between man and God, means that upon death, one's soul will be allowed to dwell in heaven with God for all eternity. A person who does not accept Christ will not go to heaven, since Christians believe Christ is the only way to God.

Please do not judge my simplistic explanations. We in the United States are very familiar with Christianity, but rarely do we have to explain it. I am merely trying to compare faiths, not criticize or disparage in any way.

Buddhist Belief

Buddhists believe in the fundamental tenets of reincarnation. As long as the person has not attained enlightenment, or has the desire for physical existence, they will continue to be reincarnated. Buddhists believe that in present and future lives, positive actions will nurture positive results. Likewise, negative actions will nurture negative results. Buddhists do not believe in the existence of God. Their fundamental belief is the enlightenment of the individual. By immersing themselves in the "Four Noble Truths" and following the "Eightfold Noble Path," practitioners of Buddhist teachings will eventually reach the enlightened state of Nirvana (Nibbana), which is a state of eternal bliss.

What I Think

The study of other religions is enthralling. God created the world and he created humans. Humans created religion.

Universal among all is the belief in an afterlife. The world we know is not the only game in town. All faith systems believe in a soul and that the soul lives forever. Most believe it is a one-shot deal, one time on Earth and the forever in the spiritual realm. Although most maintain that there is something akin to heaven, either a place or a sense of being close to God, not all proclaim there is a hell. The Hindu faith professes that the soul lives many physical lives.

Please understand that my interpretations of various world religions are my own. If you feel that they have been incorrectly stated or misleading, research them for yourself and draw your own conclusions. Checking out other religions can be a very good starting point from which to examine your beliefs, no matter what your faith.

It was stimulating research for me. I learned many details about many religions, and most dramatically, I learned one thing about myself: I can no longer call myself a Christian.

CHAPTER 5

RELIGION ≠ SPIRITUALITY

*"Fix reason firmly in her seat, and call to her
tribunal every fact, every opinion. Question with
boldness even the existence of a God; because, if there
be one, he must more approve of the homage of
reason, than that of blindfolded fear."*
—*Thomas Jefferson*

All religions are man-made, and therein is the problem.
All have some things right, some things that make sense,
but none are perfect. Only God is perfect. Religions and
religious leaders often behave as if they are speaking for
God. I believe that God is fully capable of speaking for
himself. The Koran, the Torah and the Bible all contain
God's wisdom, but sometimes people can get so caught
up in the study of the written work, they stop thinking

about God. They fall into the "trappings" of religion and lose their true spiritual connection to God. It makes me think of tourists sitting at a sidewalk café in Rome with their noses buried in guidebooks; if they would just look up, they would see Rome and its wonders all around them. If people would start looking, they would see that God is all around them as well.

Theology is defined as the study of the nature of God and religious truths. This is the basis for an organized and formal body of opinions concerning God and man's relationship to God. Each religion, and differing denominations within each religion, holds up different truths. Therefore, each religion, and each branch, forms its own particular theological doctrine. No single theology or religion seems to have all of the answers, but each has its own little piece of the truth.

Judaism

In 2000 BCE, the G-d of the ancient Israelites (followers of Judaism do not spell the title of the deity in full, out of reverence and respect, so in Jewish essays, you would see "G-d" in print) established a divine covenant with Abraham. Judaism, Christianity, Islam and the Baha'i faith all trace their roots back to Abraham and are termed "Abrahamic religions." They all are monotheistic, meaning belief in a single God. Abraham, Isaac, Jacob and Moses are revealed as prophets; Jesus of Nazareth is not accepted as the Messiah in Judaism.

By the first century CE, there were about twenty-four Jewish sects, and many anticipated the arrival of a religious, political, military figure to drive out the Romans and restore independence. Yeshua of Nazareth, as Jesus was called, did not fill the bill for most Jews. Followers of Jesus were originally considered a Jewish sect, called Jewish Christians. Paul then spread the religion to the Gentiles throughout much of the Roman Empire. Paul's movement flourished and evolved into modern-day Christianity.

The Hebrew Scriptures, now referred to by Christians as the Old Testament, make up the Jewish religious text, the Tanakh, and are divided into three groups. The most commonly known term is the Torah, the first five books, which contains six hundred and thirteen commandments. Torah means "instruction." The other groupings of books are called the Nevi'im and the Ketuvim. The Talmud is also studied and contains stories, laws and medical knowledge.

Jews are very strict monotheists—they see God as one unique entity. Most Christians view God as a Trinity: Father, Son and Holy Spirit. Jewish belief also does not accept the Christian concept of original sin. Judaism affirms the inherent goodness of people, as they were made in God's image.

Judaism recognizes the concept that Christians, Muslims and Baha'is worship a similar God. Jews also maintain that the righteous of all nations have a place in the world to come. One of the world's oldest religions,

Judaism is not even in the top ten now, as far as the numbers go.

Traditional Christian Theology

Christianity has been proclaimed as the largest religion in the world. It takes its name from the basic tenet that Jesus of Nazareth was the Son of God and the Messiah prophesied in the Old Testament as the Christ. The title *messiah* comes from a Hebrew word meaning "anointed one" or "king"; the Greek translation is *Christos,* which is the source for the English word Christ.

Christians believe that man is born with original sin and is therefore separated from God. The fundamental concept of Christianity is that Jesus is God's perfect son, and through his death on the cross and his resurrection, man can be reconciled with God and dwell with God for eternity. Christians accept that Jesus was conceived by the Holy Spirit and born of a young virgin named Mary. Followers believe that through faith in Jesus one is saved from sin and death, and given eternal life.

In the year 312, nearly three hundred years after the death of Jesus, Constantine won control of the Roman Empire. Attributing his victory to the intervention of Jesus Christ, he elevated Christianity to favored status in the empire. "One God, one Lord, one faith, one church, one empire, one emperor" became his motto. However, the early Christian Church was still plagued by deep-rooted doctrinal and theological disputes, the most contentious of which was the debate about the true nature of Jesus Christ: Was he man, God or both at once? In an effort to solve these differences and define the doctrinal faith of the Christian Church, Ecumenical Councils were held.

These councils took place in Nicaea in 325, and the powers-that-be who were in attendance drew up a declaration of faith, the Nicene Creed, which is still widely used by many congregations today. At the second Ecumenical Council in 381, Christianity was declared the official religion of the Empire, and the Creed was also slightly revised. Subsequent councils debated the doctrine of the Holy Trinity, the human versus the divine nature of Christ, and the function of icons in worship. They also deliberated and decided what writings would be included in what we now call the Holy Bible.

Christianity is pervasive throughout modern history, and even influenced how time became marked: BC, Before Christ, and AD, *Anno Domini,* which is Latin for "in the year of our Lord." Many people now prefer the use of the more neutral BCE, Before the Common Era, and CE, Common Era, to mark dates in history.

Islam

Islam, which means "submission to God," originated from the teachings of the Prophet Muhammad (570–632). The faith developed from "divine" revelations made to Muhammad, a religious and political leader born in Mecca. Annual pilgrimages are still made there by many followers. God's revelations to Muhammad were recorded in the one hundred and fourteen *suras* (chapters) and six thousand, two hundred and thirty-six *ayets* (verses) of the Koran. The Koran provides the basis for legal and judicial systems, and prescribes a pattern of daily individual and community living. Supplementing the Koran is the Sunna, which developed from the traditions, moral sayings and parables of Muhammad, and on which much of Islamic common law is based.

A follower of Islam is called a Muslim, which means "one who submits to God." Currently, Islam is the second largest religion in the world. Muslims believe that God sent many human messengers to teach the world his ways, including Adam, Noah, Abraham, Moses and Jesus. Muhammad is believed to be the last of these great prophets. Muhammad is not purported to be the founder of a new religion; he is the final prophet, the restorer of the faith that has gotten distorted over time. Islamic texts regard Judaism and Christianity as predecessor traditions to the teachings of Muhammad.

Muslims consider the Koran to be the literal word of God. The English title "Koran" is taken from the Arabic word *Qur'an*, which means "recitation." The people of the Islamic religion maintain that the written Koran is perfect only in its original Arabic. Translations are human efforts and therefore prone to human error, differences in languages, and not the original inspired text. Any translations are treated as interpretations, and not the true Koran.

The Koran includes writings about Jesus, the great prophet and teacher, a true messenger of God. Muslims do not believe in his death and resurrection, which is the cornerstone of Christianity. The Islamic name for God is Allah. Other names are used to describe his characteristics: the Creator, the Merciful and the Compassionate.

Sikhism

Sikhism was founded over five hundred years ago and today has a following of over twenty million people, making it the world's fifth largest religion. The Sikhs' word for God is "Vahiguru" and they see God as a single, personal creator, formless and eternal. They believe that before creation, all that existed was God. Sikhs believe that God is present in all creation and visibly present to those who have spiritually awakened. They believe that God is neither male nor female, and that God has created life on other worlds besides the one that we know. They also believe that all people are viewed as equal by God. The Hindu system is caste-oriented and Sikhs reject this, giving every male the middle name "Singh," meaning lion, and every female "Kaur," meaning princess.

Guru Nanak Dev founded the Sikh religion in the fifteenth century in northern India. The word "guru" means teacher. The ways of Sikhism have been formed by ten different gurus over the course of about one hundred and fifty years. Although people are welcomed into the religion, Sikhs do not try to convert people to their faith. The goal of a Sikh is to build a close, loving relationship with God. They repeat prayers throughout the day and worship together at temple. The most famous temple is the Golden Temple in India.

Sikhism is one of the most forward-thinking faiths that I have encountered from a research standpoint. Their basic philosophical tenet is that all human beings are the children of God, regardless of any particular religious belief. At the heart of their faith is devotion to God. The title "Sikh" comes from the Sanskrit and means "disciple or student," and a life of truthfulness, honesty, equality and social justice is embraced at the very core of their existence. They believe that the way you live your life is what is important, not the practice of ritual religion.

The author Pearl S. Buck read the holy book of the Sikhs, called the *Guru Granth Sahib,* and stated: "I have studied the scriptures of the great religions, but I did not find anywhere else the same power or appeal to the heart and mind, that I find in these volumes… They speak to a person of any religion, or of none. They speak to the human heart and the searching mind."

Baha'i Faith

In a similar thought pattern as Islam, followers of the Baha'i faith believe that the next prophet to come along after Muhammad was Bahá'u'lláh. Bahá'u'lláh was a nineteenth-century Persian nobleman who received manifestations of God while held captive in prison for his beliefs. Baha'is believe in one God, the same God as Muslims and Christians, the creator of the universe and all things. They also believe in the succession of a line of prophets. Similar to Muslims, Baha'is maintain that Jesus was a great teacher, but not the final prophet. According to Baha'is, Muhammad was not the final prophet, and Bahá'u'lláh could be followed by another prophet.

Their beliefs are rooted in three very basic core principles: the unity of God, the unity of mankind and the unity of religion. The Baha'is expect to inaugurate an era of peace throughout the world and through all religions. Many people today view the world's religions as opposing groups, competing against each other. Bahá'u'lláh did not see it that way. He said they were all one religion with different names. Their central truths are harmonized; the social laws, however, change according to the times. Recognizing this unity among religions will help create a peaceful global society.

God is often referred to by titles: All-Powerful, or All-Loving. The term "Baha'i" is from the Arab word *Bahá*, meaning "glory" or "splendor." Baha'i writings emphasize the equality of all human beings and they believe the unification of mankind is the most important issue in our world today. Currently there are over six million Baha'is in over two hundred countries, and it is one of the fastest-growing religions in the world.

Hinduism

One of the oldest spiritual traditions, the Hindu faith is more an approach to the universe, and a way of living in the universe. Hinduism includes a far wider range of beliefs and practices than many other faiths and does not insist on being the only truth. There is no individual who is, or has become, central to the faith and its practice.

Hinduism, generally regarded as the world's oldest organized religion, also ranks as the third largest. Hinduism differs from Christianity in many ways: It does not have a single founder, a specific theological system, a single system of morality or a central religious organization.

All of the religions previously mentioned above were monotheistic: one God. Most forms of Hinduism are henotheistic religions. They recognize a single deity, and also view other gods and goddesses as manifestations or aspects of that supreme God, called Brahman. Henotheistic and polytheistic religions have traditionally been among the world's most religiously tolerant faiths.

The primary sacred texts of Hinduism are the Vedas: the Rig Veda, Sama Veda, Yajur Veda and Atharva Veda. The Vedas contain hymns, incantations and rituals from ancient India. The Rig Veda is assumed to be the oldest of the four; estimates of its composition, originally in oral form, range from 1500 to 4000 BCE. The date when the Vedas were transcribed into written texts is not known, probably as early as 300 BCE.

The Hindu trinity of God includes the creator (Brahma), the preserver (Vishnu) and the destroyer (Shiva) of the universe. Hinduism has many, many facets. Meditation is often practiced, with Yoga being the most common. Other activities include daily devotions, public rituals and *puja,* a ceremonial dinner for a God. The New Age movement has borrowed many of its concepts from Hinduism.

Buddhism

Is the fourth largest religion in the world. It was founded in northern India by the first-known Buddha, Siddhartha Gautama. He was born a prince in 563 BCE near the foothills of the Himalayas, which is now part of Nepal. Siddhartha was raised Hindu.

He tried meditation, and deemed it a valuable skill, but stated that eventually one has to return to normal waking consciousness and face the unsolved problems of life. He tried fasting. He ultimately determined that the path to achieving the state of nirvana—a state of liberation and freedom from suffering—was to pursue a "Middle Way." This way was mainly defined by moderation in all things and included meditation.

In 535 BCE, at the age of thirty-five, it is claimed that Siddhartha developed the ability to recall the events of his previous reincarnations in detail. He was able to see how the good and bad deeds that people performed during their lifetimes led to the nature of their subsequent reincarnation into their next life. He had attained nirvana. He would never again be reincarnated into a future life. He attained enlightenment, and assumed the title "Lord Buddha" ("one who has awakened").

He then spent the rest of his life spreading the news about the Middle Way and how it is the true path to nirvana and enlightenment. Buddhism is different from all the other religions discussed because it is a religion that has no God, no Supreme Being.

Study Results

I read and researched vast amounts of information on various religions, and I prayed. My conclusion was the way I began this chapter: All religions have some things right, but for me, not one could fit all the pieces together in a way that satisfied my soul. Studying other faiths did not prompt me to convert to a different religion.

I was born and raised Catholic so to even embark upon this path of questioning seemed a little strange. I had been similar to almost everybody else, a little set in my ways. To take on soul-searching and book-researching was a daunting task, yet I felt driven. I felt it was the right thing to pursue knowledge, and in no way was it disrespectful to God. I had an innate sense that God wanted me to keep seeking and learning. Unlike Buddhists, I do believe in a Supreme Being. I am convinced that God exists.

I was not at all dismayed that I didn't find contentment within the boundaries of any one particular belief system. At the heart of all religions is the basic premise to love and do good works toward our fellow man. Why should only one religion have all of the answers?

This review of world religions only confirmed the thesis that was beginning to take shape in my mind, my heart and my soul: God is real, God is eternal and God gives us many avenues to approach him. Organized religion is not the only way.

That statement in itself may sound blasphemous to some. And maybe I am a heretic. I believe a person's faith is a very personal thing. I believe God wants a personal relationship with each of us. Traditional Christian teachings state that the only way to God is through Jesus, and I no longer believe that is the only way. It does not matter to God what "religion" a person is; what matters is their desire to seek him and to know him. A person can be spiritual without practicing any particular religion. Religion and spirituality are two entirely separate things; I have learned that I need to go where my heart leads. I am more focused on spiritual matters and feel closer to God than ever before, even though I am no longer a Christian.

Christians maintain that a deathbed confession and utterance of, "I accept Jesus Christ to be my savior" is all it takes to live with God from then on. Personally, I do not think it is quite that easy to dwell with God forever. Spending eternity in God's realm does not happen with a single "come to Jesus," but, I believe, only after many lifetimes of spiritual growth.

CHAPTER 6

THE PHYSICAL REALM AND THE SPIRITUAL REALM

"Life is not separate from death. It only looks that way."
—Blackfoot

A dear friend of mine has asked me, "Why are you so against the Catholic church?" His question implies that if a person is not totally with us, they are against us. That is not true. I am not against the Catholic church. I also do not attend services at a mosque or at a synagogue, but I am not "against" those religions or any religion. I am only against a mindless acceptance of believing whatever I am told. I am for exercising my free will, which is a gift given to us from God, and I no longer want to turn over this gift to someone else.

I want to be in charge of my own path to God. God wants me to find him; he does not want someone else to find him for me. That is what he wants for all of us.

My journey of self-discovery has happened over a course of time. When faced with the deaths of my father-in-law and mother-in-law and the loss of my job, I had a lot of questions. I realized that I needed to come to terms with my beliefs, and at that time, I was not sure myself what my beliefs were. I think I am not alone in that department.

Book Learning

My reading and researching began in earnest. Besides studying other religions, I read many books on spirituality, which, as we have discerned, is not the same as religion. The pieces of the puzzle started making sense.

God made us as spiritual beings, not religious ones. I do not envision God as a taskmaster with a clipboard, checking off that we have fulfilled our duties mandated by religious leaders. God wants us to be interested in him and to desire to know him more. Some find this in organized religion. For a long time I thought I did, but in reality, I did not. It does not make me any less or more of a spiritual being. I am not better or worse than anyone else. It is the path for me. Each person's path is unique.

The truly amazing factor is that I now know a peace that I had never experienced in this life. This state of calm is something to get excited about! How's that for an oxymoron? Because I am excited about the freedom from anxiety, and we live in anxious times, I feel compelled to encourage you to seek the same for yourself.

I think of how my father-in-law distinctly saw someone or something before he passed on; I recall the messenger that visited my mother-in-law; and I vividly see my mother speaking in tongues before she left this Earth. The obvious conclusion for me is that they were connecting with the spirit world.

We live in the physical world, but we will also live in the spiritual world. There are many books about the spiritual side of life, and I have read scores of them. Many were not any good, but some struck a chord deep within me. Books by Dr. Brian L. Weiss, Dr. Ian Stevenson, Dr. Wayne Dyer, Dr. Elizabeth Kübler-Ross and Dr. Janis Amatuzio impacted me greatly. These authors are well-respected, credible individuals from different walks of life and different areas of research, and they all arrived at a similar conclusion: We live forever.

Numerous psychics and mediums are writing books as well. I believe that some of them are scam artists, and some of them truly do have a gift. The ones who are frauds and only trying to make money ruin the reputation of those who do strive to join the physical and the spiritual realms, to ease the passage between the two planes and provide comfort for those still here. Two psychics that I believe to be truly gifted are James Van Praagh and John Edward.

If you are a person who needs hard evidence, you won't find it in this book because you won't find it anywhere. We can't prove that there is a God, we can't prove what happens to the soul and we can't even prove love, but we know that it is real. All I can offer you is advice. Ask questions and seek answers. If the questions seem endless, ask endless questions. Satisfy your own soul in its yearning for answers.

Soul Learning

This exercise is not about doubting one's faith. It is about affirming it. If you are ever asked, "What happens when you die?" you will be able to fully understand what you believe. It will give you peace on your deathbed and more importantly, peace every day in the here and now. I will ask you now to think about and contemplate what truly happens to you when you die. Have all of your spiritual teachings prepared you to honestly and seriously answer this question?

All we know is the physical world. We can't fully comprehend the spiritual world. We rely on our physical senses to literally make sense of our world, and there are still countless things in the physical world that defy understanding. We can appreciate the physical world better by becoming more in tune with the spiritual world.

As we have discovered, most people of religion believe in the soul and in an afterlife. "Death" is the process of crossing over from this physical life into the spiritual life. The soul leaves the body and is released into the spiritual world. For people of many faiths, that is it, the end. We spend eternity in heaven, in hell or in purgatory.

I have come to the realization that we are souls

inhabiting a physical body and when we leave that body, we do enter the spiritual realm. However, we do not remain there for eternity. We are not yet ready to enter the presence of God. That will require more than just a few go-rounds in the physical world.

That is why some of my Christian friends think I am off my rocker. I do not believe that one lifetime is enough for the soul to be worthy of dwelling with God. The concept of eternity is hard to grasp—literally billions of years, and that still is not all. There is no end. Trying to logically understand infinity makes my brain want to shut down. Even if we use one hundred billion years as an example, one human lifetime of seventy, eighty or ninety years is just the blink of an eye. Our entire lifetime is nothing more than a nanosecond.

Crossing Two Worlds

What we call death could be renamed "rebirth." We are eternal beings, reborn many times, not just once, onto this earth. The time spent in the physical world is used to learn, grow and evolve spiritually. There is so much to learn. The amount of knowledge that can be acquired in one lifetime is just a tiny dot in the spectrum of the universe. The duration of one natural life on earth is simply not long enough to gather enough spiritual wisdom to dwell with God for the rest of all time. Try to explain the concept of "all time." It is not an easy task. Try to comprehend the width and breadth of knowledge. No one can possibly learn everything ever, let alone in one lifetime. Attempt to define the limits of space. The universe is infinite with no beginning and no end. One can travel to the ends of the earth, but one cannot travel to the ends of space. There is no end.

So it is with God. Reading, praying and meditating have led me to encounter my truth. Heaven, as we have come to call the idea of where we go when we die (or at least we all hope we will go there) is not an identifiable place, a physical site, one we use to conjure images in our minds. It is not the "end of the road," a land above the clouds with pearly gates and streets of gold. Heaven is not exactly a location, but a spiritual realm where time is infinite, space is infinite and knowledge is infinite. It is a realm of endless growth and endless experiences.

That is the spiritual trinity: endless existence, endless universe and endless knowledge. "Heaven" can be used synonymously with "eternity." When we leave the physical world, we go to the spiritual world, heaven, eternity. In that realm, we reflect upon our past life, what we did right and where we made mistakes. There are still areas of growth to be pursued, still knowledge to be gained.

God is a God of infinite love, and because of this all-encompassing love, there is no hell. There is not a place housing a red devil with a forked tail and flames all around. We create our own hell by our actions. If the devil does exist, it is not because God created him. He was and continues to be created by the collective evil of man. There is no evil or sin in God's universe, the spiritual realm, but it does exist in the physical world.

No matter how awful a person's actions may have

been on Earth, that person was originally a soul created in God's image and that soul has potential to redeem itself. It may take many lifetimes; it is not a one-try-only crapshoot kind of life. The rationale of eternal damnation seems very harsh if you think about it—something incompatible with a loving God.

There Is No Death

We will address these issues further, but for now, I propose that most people accept that there is a physical realm and a spiritual realm. There is a point near death when the soul transcends both realms. I witnessed this with my mother. I watched in awe as she spoke in tongues to the spiritual beings that surrounded her during her last hours in this world. She was slowly slipping from our world into theirs. It was a truly wondrous event to behold.

I am confident that my mother passed into the spiritual realm and that she will again be in the physical realm. Her soul, my soul, your soul, all souls live forever. That does not mean that I did not weep at her passing. I did. The tears were not for her; she didn't need them. They were for me, because I realized what I had lost. For the remainder of this lifetime, I have to live without my life coach, my loving guide who gave me advice when I could use it, a laugh when I needed one, and a hug when I felt alone. I will miss her, her physical presence, all the days of this life until I see her again. And I will see her again, and again.

The word "death" has a negative connotation. It

brings up thoughts of finality and depression. The word does not accurately describe what is happening or what has happened. "Death" does not really exist. I encourage you to spend as much time as possible with ailing and dying family members, friends or any person, for that matter. If you actually pay attention to what is happening, you will observe a glorious transition from physical life to spiritual life that will leave you humbled and inspired.

We all know the anniversary of our birth, but none of us know the anniversary of our death. Both days pass each year, but only one is celebrated. How differently would we act or perceive this life if we knew both dates? If each year the anniversary of your death came around and you weren't really sure if this year was the final year, you would reflect, grieve, atone for sins, make your peace with God, reflect on your life and ultimately try to cleanse your soul. Knowing this date would add a new perspective to preparing for physical death and, ultimately, spiritual rebirth. Perhaps you can pick an arbitrary date, the first of the year or your birthday. If this were your last year on earth, what would you focus on? Personally, I picked New Year's Eve. Each and every New Year's Eve, I contemplate the events of the past year. If death were to come to me at midnight, would I be prepared for it? Would my family be prepared for it? Are there unsaid words that need to be spoken? Are there relationships that need mending? Can I leave this world with a smile on my face, knowing that this life was a good life?

The Eternal Journey

We are all on an eternal journey that will take us through many lifetimes and countless spiritual lessons. In the physical world, we experience, endure and hone the attributes that will nourish our soul on its journey toward God. Welcome to the soul's training ground! Some lessons may be learned in one lifetime, while other lessons will be learned over many lifetimes. Ultimately, all of God's lessons will be experienced, felt and learned.

Our journey began long before the date stamped on our current birth certificate. All of us have had many births and many physical deaths. In our present lifetime, it is a paradoxical world. The birth of a new baby is a joyous event. On the other hand, the death of someone we care about is a process laced with tremendous grief and sadness. Yet, it too is a birth.

The truth is, everyone born into a physical life will die a physical death. God has a reason and a purpose for this. We cannot merely read about grief, compassion, mercy, love, hate, hope, greed, lust, and so on. We have to experience them firsthand in our soul. God wants us to understand what it means to feel pain so we can understand what it means to cause pain. We have to be on both sides to fully understand each of these states. During a given lifetime we will know greed, and also during a given lifetime we will know what it is like to suffer from our greed or the greed of others. Only then can our soul fully understand and appreciate what greed is.

The soul is a spiritual form that experiences and learns while in the physical form. The physical world is our schoolhouse. The spiritual world is our true home. In worldly terms, the physical world is like being away at college until we can go home again to the spiritual world. We learn, we evolve, we work to sharpen our skills and then we go home to rest and reflect before our next class schedule.

Does it make any sense that given eternity, literally billions upon billions of never-ending years, we would come here for one day or even a hundred years to try to learn what it is we must learn to become one with God? Wouldn't it take countless lifetimes to even begin to understand what we must understand? Wouldn't we have to spend a life of charitable acts, a life of compassion, a life of humility, a life of service to others, a life of abundance, a life of poverty, a life of great joy, a life of great sadness? Why a single lifetime? How can we possibly experience and know all we need to experience and know in a single lifetime?

We are works in progress and we exist in time without end.

CHAPTER 7

REINCARNATION AND KARMA

"There is no death, only a change of worlds."
—Duwamish

The concepts of reincarnation and karma are not new, but they were not anything I ever gave much thought to, as they are not beliefs held by Christians. In traditional Hindu and Buddhist belief systems, karma is the total effect of a person's actions during the successive phases of the person's existence that determine the person's destiny. In Indian philosophy, karma is the influence an individual's past conduct has on his future lives. It is based on the conviction that the present life is only one in a chain of lives. The process is automatic; there is no interference by the gods. The accumulated moral energy of a person's life establishes his character, class status and disposition in the next life. In the course of a succession of lives, people can perfect themselves or they can degrade themselves to the extent that they return to life as animals. Karma and reincarnation are inseparable; karma is the force that impels reincarnation. The traditional hypothesis is that in any one life, we sow the seeds of the personality of the next incarnation. Although the concept of karma originated in India, similar ideas can be found in religions and cultures throughout the world.

In the West

Western scholars have often confused karma and fate as the same concept. Fate, however, is the belief that the path of one's life is established by forces outside oneself. Whatever happens to a person is chalked up to "destiny" or the "power of the stars." Karma is the opposite of that thought pattern. Karma is the notion that man acts with his free will, and it is his actions that create his destiny. In a nutshell, if we sow goodness, we will reap goodness; if we sow evil, we will reap evil. In modern vernacular, what goes around comes around.

A philosopher by the name of Arthur Schopenhauer is quoted as saying: "Were an Asiatic to ask me for a definition of Europe, I should be forced to answer him: It is that part of the world which is haunted by the incredible delusion that man was created out of nothing, and that his present birth is his first entrance into life."

It was not always this way of thinking, though. The concept of reincarnation is not just for the Eastern spiritual masters alone; it was an accepted logic of early Christianity and is still part of Jewish Kabbalah. Early references to reincarnation in the New Testament were deleted in the fourth century by Roman emperor Constantine when Christianity became the official religion of the Empire. Reincarnation represents a threat to the very essence of Christianity: the need for Christ's redemptive sacrifice for our sins. If we are to pay for the consequences of our sins ourselves in further lives and attain purification throughout the course of many lives, there is no need for the sacrifice of Christ on the cross.

Pythagorean Theorem/My Theory

The brilliant mathematician Pythagoras is famous for his knowledge and for the Pythagorean Theorem, one of the earliest theorems known to ancient civilizations. He was also a Greek philosopher and religious leader. He taught that the soul survives physical death and after a series of reincarnations, each one following a period of psychic cleansing in spiritual environments, becomes free eternally from the cycle of reincarnations. I am no brilliant mathematician or philosopher, but that makes sense to me.

We are a soul, housed in a body. The body does not last, but the soul continues to evolve. With each earthly life, we gain experience and we grow more knowledgeable and more spiritual. Each life can be likened to a day in God's classroom. We are learning to be like God. When one has achieved the spiritual state that complements God, no further physical births and deaths are necessary. We then stay in the spiritual world. The exception would be to reincarnate again into a physical body to help out those still on Earth. It would be a choice to return to Earth to be a guiding force to others. This is how I see Jesus—already perfect in God, but filled with the compassion to come to Earth as a teacher.

Over twenty percent of the world's population is Buddhist and Hindu, believing in reincarnation, and a recent News poll stated that twenty-five percent of Americans believe in reincarnation. The concept of "many lives" predates Christianity by hundreds of years. I think it resonates with me because this belief not only seems logical; it also tells us that God loves us unconditionally. There is no angry God passing judgment and dooming us to eternal damnation. The idea of karma is not necessarily a punishment. It is more akin to discipline, and is an opportunity for growth. It is how we bring our past negative actions and deeds into a loving and spiritual alignment. It takes many lives to get it all balanced and achieve a state of spiritual "goodness" in order to stay in the spiritual world with God for the rest of all eternity.

I was raised to believe in the Christian one-life concept. When we die, God punishes us if we have been bad and sends us to hell; or, he sends us to heaven if we've been good. We've got one chance to live and get it right, a very alarming and frustrating thought. I imagine that was what was running through my mother-in-law's mind as she lay on her deathbed. The basic tenet of Roman Catholicism is that we can never be good enough, and that is why Jesus is the only way to God.

Some evangelical and fundamental groups maintain that any belief in reincarnation is heretical and the work of the devil. I disagree. The devil is not influencing my thoughts and frankly, the only devil that exists dwells in the hearts of mankind. Satan is not a creation of God. He is real because we feed him and make him real.

There Is No Hell

The only spiritual realm is that of God, and his realm is all-loving. Any evil that exists on Earth is not God's doing. There is no devil tempting us or going to battle with the cartoon angel perched on the other shoulder. God created us in his image; he gives us his perfect love, and he gives us the gift of free will. That is where the trouble comes in.

Anyone who is a parent knows that when we give our children free will to make their own decisions, they are going to be tempted. Sometimes they make the right choice; sometimes they do not. The evil that exists in the world is from all the wrong choices being made by all of us, God's children. People create their own hell, and it literally can be a hell on earth.

I believe a human soul is always a human soul and we do not incarnate into rats or roaches. My explanation of karma is "unfinished business from one life to the next, a lesson to be learned, a wrong to be righted." We have to atone for our sins and in the process we gain knowledge and compassion and love. We grow closer to God. We become more in tune with God.

People are born into different circumstances in different lifetimes. In each lifetime we have lessons to learn or spiritual obstacles to overcome. Power, prestige and wealth are unequally distributed among individuals, and it can be because it is a consequence of actions in a previous life, or a phase of growth and achievement of a higher spiritual plane. Perhaps in a past life I was incredibly preoccupied with wealth, was selfish and greedy. In the next life, I may have to live like a pauper, always struggling for money, being forced to suffer embarrassment and humiliation. In the following life, I will have learned how to be generous and how to live a life of balance.

We are here to experience physical life in all of its elements and emotions. That is how we grow spiritually. We cannot really know suffering unless we have suffered. We cannot understand pain unless we have experienced pain; the same goes for joy, sorrow, happiness, sadness, compassion, mercy and the rest. Each lifetime is a lesson or opportunity for growth.

God knows what we experience. When we grow spiritually we reward God, and God in turn rewards us. God revels in our accomplishments, and is burdened by our defeats. God does not reward good or punish evil. If we choose evil ways such as greed, dishonesty or violence, we separate ourselves from God. Part of our growth process is to keep coming back in the physical world.

For those with great physical beauty who spend their lives trying to maintain that beauty, beauty may not be an attribute. It may be a challenge or a lesson to learn. We become distracted by our quest to glorify our looks or our bodies, when in actuality it is glorifying our souls that we should be concerned with. With each life, we tackle different areas. Imagine trying to read all the self-help books available in the library or on the bookstore shelves. In one lifetime, a person cannot accomplish every method of improving oneself: Be a better spouse, a better parent, a better worker, a better friend; manage your money, time, possessions; learn new skills; increase your intellectual capability; magnify your spiritual growth; and on and on. Build a birdhouse and learn how to do a cartwheel while you're at it.

God made us. He knows what we are capable of and in what timeframe. He does not expect us to learn everything we need to learn in one lifetime, just as we do not expect our children to learn everything they need to know in their first year of life. It requires multiple lifetimes to gain the knowledge to exist in the spiritual realm, which is God's realm. In that realm, time is infinite. God is in no hurry and his learning curve is very generous.

Why Don't We Remember Our Past Lives?

How many lives have I had already? I do not know. Why don't we remember our past lives? Simply because we are not supposed to; God designed us to live in the here and now. Nine months in the womb is not only for the creation of a physical body, but is preparation time for the cleansing or purifying of the soul. Time spent in the womb is for the development of a new life, unique from previous lives. Here, our soul, in unison with its new physical body, is set on an ongoing and evolving course. We do not get caught in a cosmic loop. Each day of our life is unique and different from every other day. During our lifetime, we will never be more pure of spirit than we are at birth. It is a fresh start.

We were not meant to remember past lives and dwell in the past. We were created by God to constantly move forward in our journey toward unity with him. This is part of the forming of our eternal soul. How could we possibly move forward spiritually if we remembered every love, every person, every hatred, every wrong, every bigoted trait, every event, every emotion from a past life? We would be unable to function in this lifetime. We would be trapped reliving our past lives over and over again. Everything God does is for our protection, and that includes protecting us from ourselves by giving us the ability to focus on just one life at a time.

Many people do have unexplained *déjà vu* moments. A memory of being in a place or knowing someone can be intense and real, or vaguely familiar, yet there is no explanation, scientific or otherwise. Maybe you have experienced this for yourself. Say, for example, you have never been out of the United States until you take a trip to Italy. When walking into a village restaurant, you have a vision or striking feeling that you have been there before when you know you have not. The eerie, gnawing feeling may fade away, yet you felt a connection. Perhaps these are glimpses into past lives.

There are many documented cases of people under hypnosis or regression therapy who can recount in great detail their past lives. There are countless unexplained but incontrovertible occasions. Why do we have such a hard time accepting the possibility? I can only suggest it is that our culture in the West is predominantly Christian, which refutes any idea except that we are born once and die once.

My conclusion is that one birth and one life is not nearly enough to be able to dwell with God. Our soul must mature to the level where it can be absorbed into the pure love that is distinctly God.

For me, it is comforting and reassuring that each of us, individually, has a truly glorious passage to God over many different, interesting and challenging lifetimes.

CHAPTER 8

GETTING LOST
ALONG THE WAY

"If you follow all the rules, you won't have any fun."
—Katherine Hepburn

The most difficult obstacle to overcome in a spiritual journey is oneself. Our human nature often feels like the Katherine Hepburn quote above. We get so tired of restrictions, and we long to break out and have fun. We want freedom. We want peace and relaxation. Believe it or not, that is what God wants for us, too.

We live in an anxiety-filled, hectic, busy world. Everyone is on the go, all the time. The rat race is named that because that is what it appears to be and often really is; we wear ourselves out pacing around, not really going anywhere at all. Many times we skip out on church, or religion, because we are exhausted or simply tired of structure and rules and mandates. Many times, we merely stop thinking about God because we are too caught up thinking about a hundred other things. We become so distracted by life and all its minute details that we squeeze out God, sometimes to the point where we think that we don't need God at all. Nothing could be further from the truth, but nothing could also be more common.

We may have been made in God's image, but we are not God. We are born human and as such, we have human faults and failings. Simply put, we are all sinners. The most basic of all human traits that keeps us away from God is that we are too susceptible to distractions. We let anything and everything take our minds off of what is really important.

Life Gets in the Way

Michael, a very close friend of mine, once said, "Life just seems to get in the way of living." How true that is. We do not live in the moment. We are always looking ahead to some magical horizon that never seems to materialize. The truly wondrous events that make up our life just pass us by as the wind on a willow. One day, we wake up and wonder who we are and how we got here. We marvel at how we have lost our way. Our life's dreams, and the noble ideas we had in our youth, have withered and dissolved with time. Our families and friends have grown older, sometimes grown apart, and sometimes grown irreparably estranged. What happened in our lives? When did we turn that invisible corner?

As we age, we realize that we can never recapture the fleeting events or moments that have passed us by. For some, a certain amount of sadness or remorse may set in over what was lost. Some of us may become disenchanted with the direction of our life, yet we are confused and we don't know what direction our life should take. We become overwhelmed by the complexity of it all. We think that all we are doing is eating up the clock. We want fun; we want meaning. We don't want an ordinary, humdrum existence.

Our lives can be exciting, fun and fulfilling if we focus on the right things. God wants us to experience the abundant joys of physical life. We can, if we learn to overcome the various hurdles and distractions that we face all throughout our lives.

Negative Attitudes

Don't let your own mindset or the outlook of others bring you down. To let yourself, or someone else, ruin the day is to let them steal a day of your life. Don't let this happen. Each day is a gift. Always be mindful of the events and people who surround you or who you come in contact with; embrace the positive, reject the negative. Studies have shown that a bad mood or negative attitude can be contagious, so be cognizant of this fact. It may take a conscious effort to pull yourself out of a negative frame of mind, but it is worth it.

Rejecting the negative does not mean abandoning or snubbing negative people. Someone has to help them see life the way it should be seen. Part of our mission in life is to coexist and work with people. Instead of ignoring or turning our backs on those who have become negative or disenchanted with life, we should, by word and deed, set an example. It is up to us to give them the spiritual boost they need to improve their lives, and to see the worth and value of their existence regardless of how mundane or meaningless it appears to them. This can be done as subtly as sharing humor to lift their spirits.

Agreed, it is emotionally draining to be around negative people for long periods of time. My suggestion is always to be positive and upbeat, even if it requires great effort on your part. Don't be judgmental, righteous or condescending. Try to help in ways that you think will be most acceptable or tolerant to the person. Gear your approach to such people on an individual basis. Everyone is different, and everyone has different thoughts, feelings or circumstances. There will always be someone who is truly negative and likes being negative; accept them the way they are, but do not let their negativity immerse you.

The Almighty Dollar

Yes, we all have to earn a living and support our families, but in the process we should not lose sight of what is truly important in our lives. Family, friends, God, humanity, nature, compassion, caring, spirituality, love—all of these should be at our very core. The rest will take care of itself.

There is nothing wrong with working hard to provide financial security for yourself and your family, or to "get ahead" in life. Just make sure you don't lose yourself in the balance. Who you are is not a trade-off for financial reward. Who you are is what you carry from this life to the next, for all of eternity.

Let me ask you this: In the long run, do you really think God cares about how much money you earned? Can you take all the material possessions you have accumulated with you into the next life? Of course not, but to study our lifestyles and our priorities, it seems we have a warped view of what really matters in life. If aliens were to land on Earth to study our culture, would they see the vast majority of humans as materialistic or spiritual?

In this life, we become exactly what we subconsciously strive to become. We are driven by the world of materialism, advertisements, mall shopping and marketers hyping the next electronic gizmo or a fancier car or a bigger house. We pamper ourselves, live beyond our means and then wonder why we never seem to have enough or why we can never get ahead. Our lives are ruled by how much income we acquire. For a lot of us, rich or poor, God is not only on the dollar bill—God is the dollar bill.

Career

As far as our careers are concerned, we subconsciously set our own self-worth by what we are willing to accept from an employer, and then we complain that we are not being paid enough, or that the job is too stressful, or that our boss doesn't appreciate us. Our work life is the career that we diligently pursued, or the one we settled for, and is based on the decisions that we have made. There is no one else to blame. We set the value on our own self-worth and we are reimbursed accordingly, both financially and emotionally. We love to point our finger at someone else or a set of circumstances that we feel have led to our shortcomings or our lot in life. The truth is that we have created our own reality by our actions, our decisions or our indecisions, and by our acceptance of events or circumstances.

Our American culture tends to define a person by his job. Often, the first question that comes up in a conversation with a new acquaintance is, "What do you do for a living?" It would be great to reply, "I live for a living." Tell someone that you are the provider for your family and then discuss your spouse, your children, your hobbies, your love of nature or whatever it is that brings you joy. Whatever our job, it is just one part of who we are; how we do that job and how we conduct ourselves in all aspects of life is the essence of who we are and how we should define ourselves. Our attitude and character is what defines us, not our career.

Fear

Our daily lives are gripped by fear. If you told this to someone in your family or one of your friends, they may look at you like you have lost your mind, but it is true and it is an avoidable, self-induced infliction.

We are afraid to take a chance. We are afraid to get married, get divorced, have a baby, buy a house. We fear rejection; we fear success. We fear boredom; we fear change. We fear new technology; we fear getting left behind. We fear we work too much; we fear we do not work hard enough. We fear we have too much on our plates; we fear we could lose our jobs in the blink of an eye. We get tangled in a web of fear that can paralyze us.

We are afraid to change jobs; we fear we will lose our house or be embarrassed in front of our neighbors. We are afraid we will not be able to pay our medical bills, or the kids' college fund, or the home mortgage or car payment. We fear not fitting in. We fear illness. We fear growing old. We fear dying. The list is endless. We become victims of our fears and they distract us from enjoying the glorious life that God wants for us. We need to learn to live without fear and without regret. God wants us to see the beauty all around us and to appreciate what we have. God desires for us to use the abilities he gave us and not let our fear hem us in.

For years I dreamed of owning my own business, but I was always afraid to make the leap. I had a wife and three children to support. What would we do if my business turned out to be a flop? I will never know, because I didn't take the chance. What is the worst that could have happened? Some financial struggle, perhaps. Maybe I was too concerned with what people would think if my business did fail. It seems ridiculous now, but I let those fears keep me in their grasp. I let fear win and the only place that the fear existed was inside of me. Fear is not a tangible enemy, but it is one of the most powerful forces on the planet.

We constantly worry about things we cannot control. Not a single day goes by that we don't worry about something. What a way to live this life that God gave us! Fear and worry create a state of being that is much closer to hell than to heaven. We have to make our life the one that God wants for us: a life of wonder and challenge; of growth and knowledge; of overcoming our weaknesses and shortcomings; of courage and self-confidence. The life that we desire is also the life that God has in mind for us. We have to make a conscious decision to rise as a champion and not lay on the canvas in defeat. We can fall vanquished or we can rise victorious.

We can get beyond our fears. Trusting in God has nothing to do with religion, but everything to do with God himself. Pray, meditate, talk to God. Take the time to be quiet and listen for God to answer. Most people do not hear an audible reply, but God can speak to you and guide you in many ways. God does not want us to live a life that is ruled by fear.

Sin

Humans are sinful creatures and our sins are many. Most religions acknowledge this fact. We all break the Ten

Commandments in various ways, but sins are anything that keeps us from God, actions that hurt our spirituality instead of enhancing it. Most the time we get too caught up in ourselves and fall to the temptations of greed, ego, lust, anger, jealousy, bigotry, intolerance or hypocrisy.

These are spiritual sins that leave marks on our souls. They involve behavior- or character-related acts, and they lead to other human faults, including all forms of lying, deception and dishonesty. Basically, we are only deceiving ourselves. We cannot hide from God. He sees our actions and he knows our hearts. It boils down to the scenario of getting too distracted by the world, and overstating or misunderstating our place in it. Some of us think we are better than others; some of us have insecurity and self-esteem issues. God wants us to love each other as he loves us. If we take our concern off of our own problems and look at our fellow man, we will see our trials aren't so bad and that there is always something we can do to help out somebody else.

The idea of each lifetime is to learn and grow more spiritual, to become closer to God. There are people in some churches who are very rigid in their beliefs and maintain that anyone who feels differently is wrong. One example is how some churches treat homosexuals. It is not a sin against God to be gay. The sin against God is hatred or intolerance toward your brother or sister. If two people truly love each other, God feels that love. In God's universe there is not any distinction between types of love. The feeling of one human being loving another is what is important to God, not sexual persuasion. In the spiritual realm, we are neither male nor female; we are spiritual entities, and love permeates to our very core.

Intolerance is a spirit-eroding sin. The longer a person continues to have intolerant views or actions, the more corrosive the effect is on the soul. Intolerance toward ethnic groups, classes of people, religious affiliations or different cultures or lifestyles breeds an animosity that will surely have long-lasting karmic repercussions.

The concept of greed also runs contrary to the laws of God and to the benefit of mankind. Greed is the basis of all conquest and wars. We all have an element of greed within us. It is up to us and our free will to control this characteristic, and not let it spiral out of control and grow like a cancer. The Egyptians, the Romans, Alexander the Great, Ghengis Khan, WWI, WWII, Korea, Vietnam, the Persian Gulf—all are based on the principle of greed. We either want what someone else has or we want the power to control or dominate them. *"They are our enemy"*; *"Let's kill them before they kill us"*; *"They don't believe in our God"*; etc., etc. Throughout the ages, the leaders of mankind have sent us to war with noble slogans and lofty ideals. The bottom line is that all wars are started by greed, pure and simple: the greed for land, the greed for wealth, the greed for power, the greed for domination, the greed to promote your beliefs over someone else's. *"Let's start a new world order."*

We may try to convince ourselves otherwise, but the root cause is greed.

On par with greed is ego. Our society worships the

rich and famous, but all of us are constantly posturing, primping and posing during our daily lives. Ego and vanity are all-consuming drivers of our daily mental vision and activities. We are more concerned about what others think of us than of what we think of ourselves. It is not just Hollywood types and the affluent; no matter our status or wealth, most of us are guilty of being on an ego trip or driven by ego. Ego is a constant companion that we must all guard against. We take our eyes off of God, and we stare into the mirror, looking at complacency.

Finding Our Focus

During this physical life, we are distracted by school, working, watching television, going to sporting or entertainment events, water skiing, bowling, yoga, skydiving, doing taxes, working on our cars, landscaping our houses, the beauty parlor, the mall, vacations, travel, playing computer games and on and on, *ad infinitum*. We have perfected the art of filling our life with distractions.

Where do we find time for God or for nurturing our soul? We don't make it a priority to fit God in. Maybe we can give him five minutes during TV commercial breaks for a quick Bible devotional reading or sit in a church pew for an hour a week. Many times during church, we let our minds wander and don't really focus on God. We spend ninety-nine percent of our time being distracted and maybe one percent thinking about God. In no other relationship would this work, and we cannot begin to assume it works with God. A person would find this kind of attitude insulting. Luckily for us, God is a God of infinite love and compassion and forgiveness.

We need to realize that we don't have to fall under the power of distractions and that we can focus our minds and our hearts on our spirituality. Our soul needs to learn and grow and expand in spiritual wisdom. We need to concentrate and listen to our inner voice. Consider what it is that God wants you to accomplish in this lifetime. Are you a good parent, spouse, neighbor, friend, worker, brother or sister? These are the important things in life. It is amazing that by concentrating on these areas, the rest of the distractions fade away, and life becomes more pleasant all around.

Stopping to Ask for Directions

We are all flawed humans. We have all committed sins and done things of which we are ashamed. No one is perfect. The good news is that it is never too late to change, to reinvent ourselves, to heal ourselves, to become the person that God wants us to be. All we have to do is tune in to our inner spiritual compass, and ask God for directions back to the right path.

CHAPTER 9

GOD, OUR LOVING PARENT

*"Remember that your children are not your own,
but are lent to you by the Creator."*
—Mohawk

My mother's love truly was a gift from God. She showed
me unconditional love and acceptance, no matter what.
Mothers have a way of blessing their children that is
special and unique. Now transfer that love and blessing
to God, and let it magnify a million times over. The
depth of love is unfathomable. As the modern cartoon
character Buzz Lightyear would say, "To infinity, and
beyond."

Anyone who has had a loving parent here on earth
knows a small taste of what God's love is like. His love
and his concern for us override all other issues. Isn't

that how we try to raise our children? We work to instill decency and compassion in them. We strive to show them a strong work ethic so they will see the value of hard work. We want them to know right from wrong and we want them to choose on the side of right. We have expectations, and we have hopes and dreams for them.

We make decisions every day based on their welfare and gear our lives around what is best for our children. When an incident occurs and we must discipline them, we do so although we silently weep inside. I have learned a piece of advice early on. When having to deal with a family issue, if we must err, it is always better to err on the side of love. Love is the strongest force on Earth and love is also the strongest force in any realm. Love is the driving force of the universe.

Giver of Life

I believe that God is the creator of all things, the giver of life and love. That was true for me even before I started my spiritual journey. I never really doubted that God loved me but honestly, I never gave it much thought. Now I think about God all the time. My spiritual eyes have been opened and I am constantly reminded of God's goodness. The easiest analogy to explain how I now see God is to view him as a loving parent. Many religions call God the "father" and claim that we are all "children of God." Those words mean something to me now. I do feel like a child of God and that as a parent he wants to give me love, protection and guidance. Some people think of God as "he." Some prefer "she." Some like to use the word "Spirit." For simplicity's sake, I will refer to God as "he" but you can insert whatever word speaks to your heart.

It is my belief that God first breathed life into every living thing, and he first loved our children before we loved them. We are God's children; so are our own kids. God has given us our children to love, to nurture, to cherish. They do not "belong" to us. I feel it is more as if God granted us custody of them for a short time here in this world. The eighteen years of a child's growing up goes so fast! Imagine what our lifetimes are like on God's scale of time!

For those of us who are parents, we have a duty and a responsibility to our children, but it is one of joy. We should share the wonder with our children and marvel with them as they grow. If we try to see the world through their eyes, we may see more of God in every corner and behind every tree. I like to think that God feels joy as he watches us grow into spiritual maturity.

As a parent, I may have a small idea of what God must feel like when he watches us, his children. We try to give our children wings and let them fly away, yet we always keep a watchful eye on them. We want to celebrate their triumphs and we want to ease their sorrows. We are connected not through DNA or blood, but through love. I delight when they delight and I cry when they cry. I imagine that God feels the same emotions with each of us.

After my years of searching, meditating and praying, if I were now asked to define God in two words, I would have to say, "loving parent." I believe with every ounce in me that God loves us unconditionally, that he does not attach strings to his love or temper his love according to our behavior. Can you imagine what that would be like? Anything you do wrong and *zap*, God does not love you today. Some people have been brought up to believe that God is in fact a cruel taskmaster and a punisher. That theory just does not work for me.

If you are a parent, think of how you relate to your own kids. At my home, we don't have a big chalkboard list of do's and don'ts and withhold our love accordingly. If you do not get straight As, I won't love you. If you are not a star athlete, I won't love you. If you do not make your bed, I won't love you. On the flip side, there would have to be a list of things to do in order to restore our love. You ate all your vegetables at dinner, *poof*, now I love you again.

I don't see God with a scoreboard. For me, God's love is complete and total and without reserve. There have been times while raising my three kids that have been challenging, and their actions have occasionally concerned me, but never has my love faded or been held over them with a mocking "I give it and I can take it away." Our human capacity for love exists because God first loved us.

My path has brought me to the point where I feel strongly that God's love is his most precious gift to us.

He loves us. That's all there is to it. It is the most plain and simple truth, yet somehow people sometimes find it difficult to grasp. His love is not contingent upon any vows to recite, any required clothing, or even that you love him in return. So if a Sunday school teacher from long ago conjures images of a mean and vengeful God, I hope you will take the time to find out for yourself what God can be for you. Don't be afraid. I know your path will take you along a different route than mine, but I also feel confident that you are going to be glad for the journey and the discoveries you make.

Take God's Hand

When I pray, I feel closeness to God. I feel a connection.

In most religions, it is agreed that God is the deity that created us. Most leaders of worship, be they priests, rabbis, ministers, *omans*, or whatever, will tell you about God's power and that God is deserving of our worship. Some denominations do preach about God's love. Some prefer other tactics. Some speakers will deliver sermons and lectures and fire-and-brimstone oratories about how you should repent: Turn from your evil, wicked ways before it is too late. They grow hoarse warning about the fires of hell, and they like to be very dramatic in their presentations.

It does not make sense to me that God would want fear to be the motivation in our life. For me, God guides with a loving hand. What kind of parent would say, "If you ever do that again, I will stop loving you"? And what kind of God would say, "If you ever do that again, I will not only stop loving you, I will send you to hell, which is the absence of all love for all eternity"?

My picture of God does not work that way because I do not think love works that way. That is not how a loving parent operates. No matter how angry or disappointed we are with our children, we never stop loving them. We discipline out of love, to help them have healthy, productive lives. We take our children by the hand and guide them when they are young. As they grow older, they may no longer wish to hold our hand, but figuratively, we still do so. We nurture them along the path until they are ready to leave the nest and move out on their own. We parents want our kids to thrive in all areas of earthly life—mentally, emotionally, financially, physically and spiritually. We teach them lessons throughout their lives to help them make it on their own. It is our goal that our children become successful, independent adults who no longer need us.

The Paradox

That is the one area where I think God's love differs. With God, it is the opposite. As we grow in spiritual maturity, the goal is to get closer and closer to God. He draws us in and wants to nurture us more and more. The more we seek God, the more we learn of his loving goodness and the more we want to experience it.

In every other way, God's love is parallel to our earthly love for our kids. Even if you do not have kids, I hope you understand my analogy: God loves us all. We are all his children and he wants us to grow deeper in love with him. It does not matter if you are a parent or not. Hopefully you had a strong, loving relationship with one or both of your parents. But even if you did not, it is my sincere wish that you have experienced love and can relate to how much more magnificent God's love is for us.

My journey has led me to today, where I am convinced that God's love is never-ending. As with the time and space continuum, God's infinite love defies explanation or understanding. We don't have to understand a rainbow or a sunset to know that it is a beautiful thing; we just accept it. The same applies to God's love. We don't have to understand how someone could love us so much; we just need to simply accept it. Once you start tuning in to God's love, you will want more of it throughout your life.

As we raise our kids, we are setting them free to make it on their own in their world. It is our goal as parents to have them become independent. We don't completely cut them loose to navigate the waters of adulthood alone, but their maturing means living without us.

As a parent, we teach our children to hold our hands for a little while, and then they have to be able to cross the street by themselves. The spiritual journey is not about preparing us how to live without God. Indeed it is preparing us to be able to dwell with him forever.

Prayer

We are always available for our children and God is always available to us. What is our access to God? Prayer. The best way to grow closer to God is to pray. There is nothing wrong with morning devotionals or evening "before I go to bed" prayers. The only catch is that you must mean them. When you talk to God, talk to him like a trusted friend, because that is exactly what he is. You can confide anything and you will not be judged. Many times we rattle off prayers like, "Bless so and so, thank you for so and so, and feed the hungry, and heal the sick, amen." Don't let your prayers become rote. That is my only word of advice.

Give God your undivided attention and your heart-felt words. Imagine if every night you came home from work and didn't even look at your wife, or talk to her, or show any interest in her at all. Then right before you fell asleep, you mumbled, "I love you, good night." The next day, the same thing. No attention, no appreciation, not a thing. Then at bedtime, you burbled, "I love you, good night." And maybe you even meant the words. What do you think your wife would say? Would she feel loved? Would she ever know that your love for her was real? We would not expect that such little effort would indicate a real interest in a person, so we should not expect that it indicates a real interest in God. Many of us live like that, though. If we throw up a word or two of thanks, or recite a prayer from our childhood, we think we can check that obligation off the list.

A daily prayer should be a time for you to seek God, not try to appease him to keep him off your back or to try to earn brownie points. I do recommend a time of daily prayer. Most religions would agree with me there. I also am not against saying the same prayer if it has meaning for you. "Now I lay me down to sleep" probably is not it. I have a prayer that I wrote myself and when I say the words every day, I think about them and reflect on my life and God's amazing love. It has helped my spiritual journey not become a repetitive habit.

I say my psalm in the morning and it helps me concentrate my attention on God and not on me. We live in a me-centered world and taking the internal spotlight off of me and putting it on God helps me to see God in little things throughout my day; and, it helps me be a blessing to other people. If I am seeking love and calm and peace, then I won't bite the head off my coworker who messes up our project or I won't lash out at my children or spouse for a silly, inconsequential thing. Think about how often we get riled up about something and then when we look back, we think, *Wow, why did I get so upset over such a small thing?* It happens all the time. We get caught up in the stress of the world and it can eat us up. The best anti-stress device on Earth is a time of daily prayer.

Give it a try. Talk to God the way you talk to your best friend. Find a place and a time that can be your meeting place. Maybe it is your front porch, maybe it is when you walk your dog, maybe it is a quiet corner of the house, or maybe it is when you are hiking, camping or sailing. You can pray out loud or internally. I also challenge you to write a prayer of your own. It can be very simple, or it can be very eloquent. No matter your style, it is very personal and between you and God alone. Prayer should be an intimate thing. Because mine is something I have shared only with God, I am hesitant to include it in this book, but I think I will later on, only to provide an example for you. Mine works for me. Yours can be as distinctive as you are, or you can use mine if you decide you like it.

A personal prayer is like a calling card announcing to God, "I'm here." I think God smiles when he hears my prayer every day because he looks into my heart and sees that I am sincere in my desire to seek him. Isn't it a wonderful gift when one of your children calls you just because they wanted to talk to you? They didn't want any favors or want to borrow anything. They just wanted to talk. Many of us make the first move to God when we need something. I think he is okay with that and I think that he also looks forward to continuing conversations with you when the crisis has passed.

Think of how you would feel if your children never visited you. Or if they opted to send someone in their stead to wish you a happy birthday. "Jack is busy, but he really does love you and sends his best wishes." Do you think God wants someone else coming on your behalf or praying on your behalf? If you are sitting in a house of worship and the leader is praying, just because you are there, it does not automatically count as your prayer. It is a truly marvelous feeling to lift your voice to God along with countless friends and neighbors. However, it is just as marvelous to lift your solitary voice in an intimate and personal way. Whether in a group or alone, pray with respect and sincerity. Let God know you care.

You don't have to follow a mandated prayer ritual. You do not have to gather with others at a certain time. You don't have to wear anything special, say anything special or learn a special language. Just be you. Seek and you will find. Tap into God's love and watch: Your life will evolve in extraordinary ways.

CHAPTER 10

GOD'S GIFTS

10

"When we blindly adopt a religion, a political system, a literary dogma, we become automatons. We cease to grow."
—*Anaïs Nin*

The First Gift

What I have learned: God's greatest gift to us is his love. Because of his love, we are able to love others and to feel the joy of being loved back.

I think God shows his love by giving us lots of different ways to love. Love is boundless and unique between each set of parties. My relationship with my mother was separate and apart from her relationship with my siblings. She loved us all incredibly and she loved us all as individuals. She understood that each of her children loved her and that each would display that love in their own way. What a boring world it would be if we were all cut from the same cloth and reacted to everything the same way and expressed ourselves the same way. What a creative God to make us all so different!

Some people show their love very demonstratively, hugging and kissing. Others like to make people laugh. Some show their love quietly by taking care of things without being asked. Every one of us is unique and we all show all our love in our own ways. That must be how God designed us.

I think that God knows each one of us, and knows if we are serious or silly or scared. He knows our person-ality and he wants us to be ourselves. God sees that a poet and a carpenter are equal. God wants us to express our love for others and to him in our own way. That is, in a nutshell, the whole point of this chapter. I think God wants me to express myself in this way, writing this book, telling you about my search for him in hopes that you, too, will go looking for God. Your conclusions may differ, but all I want is for you to think for yourself.

I came to a point in my life where the questions were outnumbering the answers, and the only thing that made sense was to find out for myself. My journey has brought me to my convictions and I feel a peace and a happiness that I did not know before. It seems like the right thing to do to share my joy and my overwhelming need to let you know that God loves you and wants to show his love to you in ways that are special only to you. The way for that to happen is for you to make your own spiritual journey. I can tell you about mine, but yours will be yours alone. No two journeys will be the same.

The Second Gift

God loves us so much that he gives us the free will to choose if we love him back. We do not have an inborn computer chip programmed to walk and talk and worship in a set way. We are not on automatic pilot, going through the motions of life. I can't imagine that God wants a *Stepford Wives* way of relating.

Just as our children are not predestined to follow our every command, we are not some kind of "God-robots." Really then, what would be the point of existence at all? Picture the scene at your house at breakfast. Your kids file into the kitchen with shiny faces and perfectly pressed clothes. No rumples, no bad attitudes. They eat whatever you put on the table before them and say in unison, "Thank you. That was delicious." Then before they head out the door, they give a kiss to your cheek, and smile with, "Goodbye. Have a good day. I love you."

Admittedly, once in a while, that might be nice, but every day, morning after morning, it would ring hollow. We want genuine conversation and interaction with those we love. I believe God wants the same with us. The buzzword lately in certain circles is "authentic." Be authentic. Live an authentic life. It may be overused, but the sentiment is accurate. Be yourself, and in your own way, love those around you. In your own way, find God.

That, I think, is the real problem that some people have with my "conversion" away from organized religion. They do not know how to accept anything other than what they are told. They do not know how to start their own search. And yet, it is really this simple: If you have a question, go find the answer that satisfies you. You will know in your heart if it is the right answer. Your spiritual compass will point the way.

This next sentence is very important: *Everyone should know why they believe what they believe.* If you stand up and say, "I am this religion and I believe this," you should know what that means. Examine the details, and be able to explain them. To examine every detail is not questioning your faith; on the contrary, it is strengthening it. In the process, I guarantee that you will come away knowing more about yourself, more about God, and more about your faith and belief system. Nothing but good can come from such an examination.

I am not here to debate the merits of one religion against the other. If you have found God in your organized religion or denomination, I am delighted. As long as it is right in your gut, and in your heart, then I am happy for you. Finding God on our own terms means finding him on his terms, not the prescribed ways of the world.

The challenge is to seek. Too many of us follow the status quo, and we do so for many reasons. We don't give God much thought, and putting in time at the house of worship is good enough. Or we fear that God will be angered if we have questions. Or we don't want to upset our family and friends if we question things. They sometimes take it personally and think it is an attack against them if you do not believe what they believe. That is the ultimate sadness in this world. It also hits the nail on the head when dealing with some of the unrest between so many countries. We can't understand why someone cannot believe what we believe. So we want them to be like us or to disappear. We think we are the only ones who can be right.

I don't feel that way. My belief system is right for me. I also respect your beliefs. Maybe there would not be so much war in the world if we could follow that path. And it is not just world cultures that have trouble accepting each other. America is a hotbed of religious battles. Denominations are separating and forming their own churches every day. Many times the line they draw in the sand is trivial or downright against the grain of love, and I think that is what God is trying to teach us.

This church accepts gays, so a new church breaks away. This church accepts women as leaders, so a new church breaks away. This church puts an electric guitar and a drum set on the altar, so a new church breaks away. People stop thinking about God and get caught up in their petty differences of opinion. We only want to sit with those who share the same narrow views instead of seeing how much we can learn from each other and offer each other if we let our diverse views come together to worship the one great God.

If we really think about it, regardless of our religious or philosophical differences, one common thread unites us all: our love for God. And we are all on the very same spiritual journey: to find God. What a wondrous journey it is—men and women coming from different places and different times, all on different spiritual paths, yet we all arrive at the same destination. Humanity, standing together on God's doorstep. All of his children united in universal love. What parent would not love that?

Open Your Gifts

God loves me and God loves you. He also loves women, homosexuals and people who like rock music. He loves Asians, Caucasians and Lithuanians. He does not dole out love based on skin color, eye color or hair color. God's love encompasses every one of us. We often seem to have trouble accepting that fact.

God is patient with us. I sure think so, anyway. He has all eternity, but my advice to you is: Don't wait. If you have any inkling at all to start a search for God, please don't hesitate.

Life is a beautiful gift. And responsibility comes along with this gift.

I think that maybe some of you may be at a point in your life where you are doubting if life is indeed a beautiful gift. Let me offer this: If you think that you live a mundane life, you probably are right. You know your life better than anyone else. If you want to make changes, then make them! You should always strive to improve your life, but don't wait for tomorrow. Start today, but also *enjoy* today!

The point is to be happy with the life you are living. Remember to live in the moment.

Don't try to be someone you are not and don't try to live a life that you don't have. Be happy with who you are. Don't let regrets or wishful thinking rob you of happiness or paint you into a corner. Cheer for each breath that fills your lungs!

It does not cost a thing to take a walk in the park, or to skip a stone across the water or to play a game with your children (or grandchildren). Take time to bond with those you care about. By focusing on God and on the people in our lives, our problems are more easily managed, and it is easier to keep our perspective. Life will not always be easy, but it can be beautiful.

It does not matter who you are or where you live or what you do as your occupation. The richest person on Earth cannot buy a sunset. Find the joy. It is right in there with the mundane. The best way to find excitement in your life is to get excited about living.

I can tell you that you need to open your eyes and keep your senses alert. It would be easier if God displayed a large, flashing neon sign, but that is not how it works. God does not use flashing signs or, for most us, burning bushes.

He uses invisible strings that pull on our hearts and wondrous mysteries that stir our souls.

CHAPTER 11

ME AND YOU AND GOD

11

*"In religion and politics, people's beliefs and convictions
are in almost every case gotten at second-hand, and
without examination, from authorities who have not
themselves examined the questions at issue,
but have taken them at second-hand from other
non-examiners, whose opinions about them
were not worth a brass farthing."*
—*Mark Twain*

I titled this chapter "Me and You and God" because I
believe that God cares about me, and he cares about you
and he cares about all of his children. I am not so sure
that he cares about the size of our houses, our retirement
accounts or our golf handicaps, although some golfers
may be disheartened to hear so.

If you are a Baby Boomer like me, let the golden years really be a time of purpose. Whatever your age or place in life, let your years be a time of purpose, too. Let's focus on relationships. Let's focus on spiritual matters. When you do, other matters don't blow up out of proportion.

Let's focus on me and you, me and God and you and God.

My Background

I was born in the mid-1940s in Cleveland, Ohio, into a working-class Catholic family. My father was a mechanic by trade, and my mother, the family homemaker. We were a typical Midwestern family and I had a typically wonderful childhood. I have three brothers and one sister. As children, we were encouraged to play together and always to take care of each other. My siblings and I still enjoy a close and warm relationship today. Our parents cultivated that and we have done the same with our own children.

Growing up in our blue-collar family, we didn't have a lot of material possessions. We wore hand-me-down clothes. Our most prized possessions were our baseball gloves and our bicycles made from various parts of other bicycles. But life was good. Our mother was very caring and did everything she could for us. Our father worked hard his entire life to provide a good home for us.

Every summer we would all pile into the family car and drive to Florida for vacation, where we would stay at Aunt Rosie's house in Orlando. Five kids, two parents, and sometimes an uncle would make the trip in one car. I have great memories of those trips and our time together as a family.

After my typical teenage years and a stint in the navy, in 1968, I married the only wife I have ever had in this life, Phyllis. Together we've raised three beautiful and interesting children. I tell you my background so that you can see I am an average man with an average life. Most of us are average. I don't believe that fame or fortune matters in God's eyes, or earns those folks any more "God points." Most of us lead typical lives with typical families and typical jobs.

We go through each day and sometimes feel that it really can be the "same old, same old." I don't think God intended for us to have a mundane, dreary life. I admit to, at times, feeling as if I were stuck in a rut. I was raised Catholic and went to church regularly. It was part of the routine of my life. Nothing is wrong with routine, and it can be very comforting. I was jolted out of my routine, and here I am today, an average man, writing a book about how God has opened my eyes. Don't think that he won't do the same for you. Your story will be unique, and just as fulfilling.

The Seed Is Planted

When my wife's parents died within a few months of each other, my questioning began in earnest. The fact that Buddy became alert and fixated on someone or something just before he died intrigued me. What was he looking at? Did he see visions or people? Were his parents there, welcoming him into the spirit world? Was he witnessing his life flash before him? What really happens in the moment that we leave this world and go to the next?

My mother-in-law's spiritual visitor fascinated me. Her fear of death also completely puzzled me. Perhaps my own mortality entered my mind. As most Baby Boomers are beginning to realize, I am not going to stay on this Earth forever. I think most of us start to wonder at some point.

Also, during the same time as their deaths, I was laid off from my job as sales manager, and I thought it was a tragic event. As many people my age can relate to, the era of downsizing has affected many of our lives, including the lives of those around us, not to mention our egos and images of self-worth. I started to ponder the big questions of life: Is this really all there is? What do I really know about God? What happens next? That was the big one: What happens next?

The time off from work and the break from the daily grind turned out to be a blessing in disguise. It allowed me the time, peace and tranquility to reconnect with myself and to discover things about myself that had been lost over the years.

Good things came of what I thought was one of the worst events of my life: compassion for all living creatures, a humble reflection of my responsibilities as a husband and a father, and a true desire to seek God wherever I might find him. This job loss was not a bad thing, after all. I was free of the daily distractions that had been consuming my time and my soul. It gave me an opportunity to slow down and take a spiritual deep breath.

I realized how much of an emotional and personal investment I had in my career and in my working life. Many of us get caught up in our jobs, almost to the exclusion of all else. Earning a living and financial security are of course important, but they should not define a person. This forced time off gave me the break to focus on what really was important in my life. I came to see that my soul, my spirituality and my family should be at the top of my list.

I could have kicked and screamed and hated the corporate world, and believe me, I had thoughts on that wavelength, but I sat in my church pew one morning and the questions swirled in my head. It was sort of like a kick in the pants and a "well, what are you waiting for?"

My butt left the church pew, and my mind became more engaged than ever before in spiritual matters. I started reading. Seriously reading. I read countless books on religious and spiritual topics. I offer you a suggested reading list at the end of this book. I read, I analyzed, I contemplated, I meditated and I prayed; that was my process. I went looking for God, not religion, and I found the serenity and universal love that had surrounded me, but that I had been ignoring. Losing my job was a gift.

There is no present like God's love, and no time like the present, so I urge you to start your quest. You don't have to have life-jarring events to prompt you on your path. Sometimes all it takes is reading a simple book.

Whistle While You Work

Hopefully you have a job that you find rewarding, but even if you don't, the way you perform that job can be a blessing to others. Everything we do every day of our lives is an opportunity to experience growth.

I learned to not let a job become such a weight on me that it destroys who I am inside. I learned to treat my coworkers with respect. We all face challenges in our lives, and working day in and day out is hard enough without adding a disgruntled coworker to the mix. My advice is to be a friend at work, not an adversary. Avoid the gossip, the cliques, the mean-spirited teasing, or other rude or intolerant behavior. Be the person that puts a smile on coworkers' faces. Be someone they like to be around. It has made a tremendous difference in my life.

Family Ties

One of the most profound ways that God shows us his love is through our families. It is also an awe-inspiring way to grow spiritually—taking care of a family. In doing so, there will be tests to your patience, your stamina and maybe even your faith. Raising a family or caring for other family members is an act of love and selflessness. God is the supreme example of such love, and whatever we do here in this life with our families is just a taste of what the spiritual realm holds.

Getting along with family, be it your spouse, your parents, your children or your siblings, is the trickiest of waters to tread. These are the people closest to us and the ones who are the most sensitive to our actions and words. Maintaining healthy relationships is work sometimes, but it is worth it. Of all the people to whom we should spread God's love, it is our family. Growing together in love and harmony can be one of the greatest spiritual adventures that we can experience in the physical world.

All of the daily acts that we perform—be they with family, friends or strangers, or perhaps on the job—everything we do, regardless of its insignificance to us, is an act of love. No matter your family situation or profession or occupation, you can be a conduit of universal love.

Love Is All Around Us

Once you become open to true spirituality, you go through a kind of metamorphosis, and you realize that you are not alone. A great calmness comes over you at the realization that God is real, his love is real, and your life is a progression toward God. Don't get me wrong—"bad things" can still happen to you. The physical world is a place of upheaval, turmoil and random events. When bad things happen (and they will), we have to make a conscious and focused effort to reaffirm our spirituality and know that ultimately, in God's universe, everything will turn out fine. There will be good and bad, ups and downs, happy times and sad times. It is a roller-coaster ride at times, but it will strengthen your soul. Faith is not built by happy times; faith is built by trial. In street slang, faith is knowing that God has your back.

Don't squander this lifetime worrying about petty things. Don't walk in fear, don't get lost in distractions. Don't underestimate your strength as a person, and as a spiritual being.

I maintain that God's single greatest gift to us other than his eternal love is free will. Take this gift, and use it wisely. Don't by proxy turn it over to someone else to let him or her interpret God for you. No one can do your spiritual thinking except you. He meant for each of us to find the answers. Don't let someone else give you their version.

On that same note, don't try to convince anyone of your version. Everyone needs to find God in their own way and with their own heart. Free will is not the absence or lack of will; it is the homing beacon that God instilled in each and every one of us.

Don't Worry

Don't worry if things still seem fuzzy or if everything is not crystal clear. Anyone who is involved in pursuing his or her spirituality is on the right path. However, to search for or seek God is better than letting your life blow by while you spend your time searching through the *TV Guide*. Each step you take down the path gets you closer to God.

Your eternal soul thanks you eternally.

CHAPTER 12

MAKING SENSE OF THE SENSELESS

12

*"We are not human beings on a spiritual journey.
We are spiritual beings on a human journey."*
—*Stephen Covey*

I read a local newspaper account of a woman we'll call Mary, who was celebrating her eightieth birthday. Her daughter, her granddaughter and her infant great-granddaughter gathered with her for a lovely luncheon at Mary's favorite restaurant to mark the special occasion. Four generations of women together, sharing memories of past birthdays and making plans for the newest member of the family. On the way home, they were involved in a car accident. All four were killed.

How can such a tragedy happen? Why? Does God allow it? Does God cause it?

Bad Things Happen

Many of us struggle with these kinds of questions. We read the papers, we watch the news on television and we have events that occur in our own lives. It seems sometimes that the only news is bad news. People die every day in senseless and mind-numbing ways. There are automobile, airplane, train and boating accidents. People drown; there are tornados, earthquakes, floods, hurricanes, lightning and fires. Some people are riddled with disease, illness and handicaps. There are murders, a precious life taken by another person, in every imaginable and senseless way.

We are faced with uncertainties that are difficult to make sense of; we wonder why; and we ask if God caused these bad things to happen. We want to scream, "Why, God? Why me? Why my family?" We feel confused. "How could you do this to us?" If you have experienced pain and want to rage at God, go right ahead; I think he can take it. It is also my declaration that God did not cause your pain.

The physical life is not exempt from pain and suffering. Every one of us, even the most spiritual person, will feel sadness and experience grief. It is part of being human, and we really should not expect otherwise. This world can be violent, and it can sometimes seem to be a heartless place. When a senseless death occurs, it can leave behind inconsolable, grief-stricken loved ones. Their grief is tangible, and everyone expresses their sorrow differently. It is normal for a survivor to become physically and emotionally sick to his or her very core, to have trouble thinking, speaking or even breathing. It can feel like the world has spun out of control and has crashed in on top of them, crushing them.

Conflicting thoughts battle within our brains: Is it God's will that these tragic events take place? Is it God's punishment? Does God need more souls in heaven? Or are they random and tragic accidents? How do we make sense out of such senseless and devastating tragedies?

This world, the physical world, is not a perfect world. Bad things do and will happen; horrific, tragic things will and do happen. We often ask: Why does it have to be that way? Why can't a loving God just let us exist in bliss and happiness throughout our existence?

Spiritual Growth

I believe that God does want us to be happy, and that is why he gives us the experience of physical life. Each lifetime is an adventure, and an opportunity to grow. Tragic and nonsensical events are sometimes part of the package. Physical death, although difficult, is an opportunity to grow in spirituality and compassion. Everyone and every living thing you know and love will physically die, and ultimately, we will be witnesses to our own physical deaths.

Over a period of months, I watched a young father deal with the progressive and fatal illness of his only child, his daughter. It tore my heart out, and I marveled at the courage he and his wife showed under such an unimaginable weight. Losing a child is certainly a time when one needs to feel the comfort of God's love. The death of a child is a burden I thankfully have never had to bear.

It is my fervent belief that God does not deliberately send misfortune and grief our way as a form of punishment. He does not create the tragedies, but he does not stop them, either. I am sure there were a lot of very spiritual people on board the *Titanic* who were praying fervently to be saved by God as the ship sank. Was God ignoring them? I think not. I believe that God knew something we did not. He knew that their spirits would be safe, and that is what truly matters. He knew they would live again both spiritually and physically. All we know is this life, so to try to comprehend another life is very difficult, but I believe that we are eternal beings and that this lifetime is not all there is. It makes physical death easier for me to accept. During the course of writing this book, several close friends have passed on. Yes, I am saddened that I will not have their company anymore in this life, but I feel reassured that we will be reunited.

That does not diminish the grief that some people feel. Next to unconditional love, inconsolable grief is the greatest emotion, because love is at the very crux of what is driving the grief. Some may say that hatred is the second strongest emotion after love, but I believe that any hatred would wither when compared with the depths of someone's grief. Our grief is proportionate to our love. Someone or something we held deeply special in our hearts has left us. Of course, that is a difficult circumstance to bear.

Losing a loved one can sometimes be a time that tests a person's faith in God and their faith in themselves, because it gets down to the root foundations of their beliefs. I did not come to my conclusion overnight, or with the reading of just one book, but I believe with every fiber of my being that we are in fact eternal, and any pain and suffering is only temporary, and joy and love are eternal.

Love Is Eternal

Anyone who has ever lost a loved one knows that the love lives on forever. When my mother died, I missed her terribly. I wept. I want to suggest to you that although you will miss that person, and you will weep for yourself for your temporary loss, you do not need to lament that all is lost, because nothing could be further from the truth.

It is normal and healthy to grieve for ourselves because we miss our loved ones, but we do not need to feel sympathy or grief for those who have gone on to a spiritual life. They are being bathed in the warm, healing glow of spiritual love.

It is my utmost conviction that God knows that whatever pain we are going through, however great, is only temporary, and ultimately, we will be strengthened by our faith in him and by our unwavering courage in the face of these senseless tragedies. God is always our loving parent, and I believe that he sends spiritual beings to surround and comfort us. Many people believe in guardian angels; I believe that there are spiritual beings, call them whatever you choose, who exist here in the physical world. The more in tune we get with our spiritual nature, the more we feel their presence.

As parents, we have watched our children suffer grief through the loss of a beloved pet or a friend at school, or some other horrific act that was beyond our control. All we could do was comfort them and let them know that eventually, they would smile again, they would laugh again and life would go on. This is the same lesson we should also learn as adults. Although the grief and suffering may be with us throughout our lifetime, it will eventually lighten. Our soul has been marked, but not broken. Have you wept at a funeral, and laughed at a birthday? Those are the two sides of everyday life. There will be times of great testing and times of great joy. When bad things happen, and they will, do not focus on the dark side of life. Focus also on the bright side of living. If a loved one passes, regardless of the circumstances of their passing, embrace their memory and remember them for the love you shared, the joy you felt, and consider the thought that you will most definitely see them again.

Angels Among Us

In the physical world, events happen when your soul seems tested to its very foundation. You can lie on the canvas beaten down and dejected, or you can get up and use the spiritual essence that God put inside of you to triumph over the worst possible evil that has befallen your life. You can scream at God, or you can call on God and his hosts of angels to help you in your time of distress. It is my mission to tell you that they will come. If you can muster the strength to see through your grief and focus on those spiritual beings surrounding you, you will feel their strength, and you will know that you are not alone; you are never alone.

As one of God's children, you will always be in his heart and he in yours. Your reward will be that you have triumphed over occurrences that would have broken many, and you will truly be a stronger spiritual force as a result. Once the initial shock and grief have subsided to a level where you can clear your mind, it is my hope that you will come to realize that we are all eternal and that your loved one is in the spiritual realm. In that world, there is no pain, no suffering—only the bliss of witnessing God's universe and the majestic wonders he has laid out before us.

I Know This to Be True

I know this to be true as much as I know my own physical life to be true. We are eternal, absolutely and unconditionally. God created us to be with him forever. I hope that you will never doubt that you are eternal; never doubt that you were chosen by God to be with him. And above all, never, ever doubt the fate of your loved ones who have passed from physical existence; never doubt that they are safely in God's spiritual realm.

Pain and loss are overcome by love and rebirth. Each and every one of us is reborn time and again, and we will share multiple lives together. We will share new experiences, new adventures and new growth, both together and apart. We have all of eternity, a never-ending time to enjoy each other and to grow both spiritually as individuals and joined together as the fabric of God's spiritual world. Once you embark on your own spiritual journey, I am confident that you will come to the same conclusion that all of the words I have spoken are true. You, too, will rejoice in the knowledge that we will experience joys and bliss that are unimaginable to the physical human mind.

Maybe you are thinking that my beliefs are a little "out there." I understand that. How can I be so sure that we live forever? Because all of the information I have looked at for the past fifteen years, coming from many different sources and different directions, points to the same common theme: We are eternal. There is evidence of people receiving messages from loved ones who have died. There is evidence of metaphysical events occurring that point to dimensions and realms beyond our own. There are unexplainable acts and miracles that occur each and every day, from large to small. Once you start reading and searching on your own journey, I think you, too, will see that the evidence of our eternal existence is overwhelming and conclusive. It is there for everyone to find if one chooses to start looking for it.

At the end of this book, I have included a list of suggested reading, which will point you in many different directions. Pick up the scent that strikes you, and follow your path. Once I started reading and researching, I could conclusively say that intellectually, I believed what I read to be true, and in my heart, I knew it to be true. I am a child of God and I am an eternal being. I will live many physical lives before I dwell forever in the spiritual realm.

What Do You Know to Be True?

It is my wish that you start down the path to spiritual truth. I recognize that some highly intelligent people are atheists, and I admit that it bewilders me. To choose not to believe in God or God's creation is their choice, and I am amazed at how strongly I wish that everyone would come to find God, but it is their choice. I know that I will never convince them otherwise, and I wouldn't try. By the same token, they will never convince me that I am wrong. I do wonder what thoughts go through an atheist's mind as he draws his last breath. Maybe, "Gosh, I sure hope I am wrong!" Death does not frighten me because I feel it is one step closer to God.

We will all eventually die and pass through the gates of physical death, wrapped within the cloak of our own spirituality. Most of our lives, we have been taught to fear death. Many people fear death because they assume it is something they will face alone. We were not born into the physical world alone and we will not be born into the spiritual world alone. Death is rebirth into the spiritual realm. By concentrating on that thought, death should not be feared—it should be celebrated!

Physical death is the great equalizer. Whether rich, poor, famous or infamous, the only sure thing that every human has in common with each other is, in each lifetime, we are born and we will die. It is what we do in actions, deeds and apathy that will define our life. We don't all have to be famous or wealthy, and most of us will not be given either of these gifts of responsibility. How we lived, and our interaction with God's natural world, will be our legacy. Each lifetime will leave an imprint on our soul.

In a journey and an evolution that will span many lifetimes, physical birth is only half of a circle. Physical death, the passage to the spiritual realm, is the completion of that circle.

CHAPTER 13

DISCOVERIES THROUGHOUT MY JOURNEY

13

"Everyone is on a spiritual path;
most people just don't know it."
—Marianne Williamson

My journey for spiritual truth began in 1991, and for the past fifteen-plus years my eyes have been opened, and my heart has as well. My intense devotion to researching religion and spirituality has brought me to these beliefs and conclusions. If they seem strange to you, that is perfectly okay with me. Your own path and your own journey will point the way for you. Follow your heart, and make up your own mind. God will reveal his truths to you.

It does not matter who is right and who is wrong; it

only matters that we truly seek to understand who God is, who we are and our spiritual relationship with each other. Start your own journey, and never be afraid of what you will find. To seek the truth is a noble endeavor, and having the courage to seek God's spiritual truth is what I believe he wants for each and every one of us.

If you choose only to study your particular faith, go for it! Read and research everything you can on your particular faith. It can only strengthen your knowledge and your resolve in your beliefs. Search however you choose to search. God will be waiting for you at the turn of every corner. You already know of my basic beliefs that God is real, we are eternal and we are born into the physical world time and again.

My quest has led me to these other spiritual truths that I have personally come to believe along the way, and I would like to share them with you. It is not my goal to persuade you of anything. In fact, I am aware that many people do not agree with me. My intent is to show you that many issues will come to you in new ways as you start to open your mind to the possibilities that perhaps God is trying to whisper in your ear and now, for the first time, you are ready to whisper back.

Does a Rooster Crow in Heaven?

In Christian belief, the notion that there is a difference between the soul and the spirit is fairly commonplace. Many believe that every living thing has a soul, but only humans can be spiritual or have a spirit. The soul is part of the makeup of every living thing and is the essence of that being, the mind, or the thinking part; the soul can die with the body.

The supposition is that having a soul is different than having a spirit. Having a spirit means being spiritual as a way of recognizing God, or having the ability of practicing religion, or understanding the moral laws behind the fundamental nature of our existence. Only man can do that. Only man can be eternal because of his spirit; only man was created in God's image and is therefore the inheritor of God's heavenly kingdom.

What I have come to believe is that this difference in terminology is a theological contrivance of man and is based upon concepts of religion, not considerations of God. Personally, I do not make a distinction between our eternal souls and our eternal spirits, and I don't believe God does either. Animals are spiritual beings also created by God. I feel a closeness with my pets, as many people do, and I believe that animals exist with God in the spiritual realm.

I do not feel that it is man's place to understand or approve of the relationship between God and his creations of nature. I believe that God gave us dominion over the animals of the Earth; he did not give us the right to practice lordship over their souls, or to decide who or what is worthy of heaven and who or what is not.

God communicates with animals in a way hidden from man, and this is part of his design and his creation. Animals and creatures of nature are spiritual in a way *ordained* by God. I believe that giving man dominion over the creatures of the Earth and the seas was a gift of responsibility, not a right of abuse or practice self-promotion.

To answer my own question, yes, I believe that a rooster does indeed crow in heaven. According to the portion of the Bible that is accepted by several religions, God sent Noah to make sure the roosters would always continue to crow here on Earth also. I envision that God enjoys the sound of crowing roosters, barking dogs, meowing kittens, roaring lions and the howl of the wolf. After all, he gave all creatures of nature their voices.

Cults

"That one may smile, and smile, and be a villain."
—*William Shakespeare, Hamlet*

Cults prey on people who are disenfranchised from organized religion, or people who are lonely and want a place to belong. It saddens me that cults still exist, and that people still get caught up in them, quite often with tragic results. Usually a cult has a charismatic leader and takes advantage of "lost" souls. Do not turn your search for God over to anyone else. If someone tells you they are Jesus or God, run!

Please do not let anyone exercise spiritual control over you. Listen to your intuition and your common sense. If something does not feel right, then for you, it is not right. From what I understand about the workings of cults, it is easy to fall under the spell of enigmatic people who preach the word of God as a modern-day John the Baptist or a spiritual Pied Piper.

God has always been here and he will always be here. Take your time on your spiritual journey. You do not have to be in a hurry to join any group without first checking them out thoroughly. It is easier to check them out from the outside, rather than checking them out from the inside. Take a really good look before you leap. You can check with local law enforcement or government agencies. Talk to family, friends and loved ones who have your best interest at heart before joining a religious group. If anyone around you has concerns, take their counsel seriously. Those people who you have known and can trust are truly looking out for your best interests, and they will not steer you wrong.

While you are seeking information on a group that may or may not be a cult, you can continue to go to a house of worship of a known religion, and practice your faith as you want to practice it. If the leader of the new group has problems with that, that is a serious red flag. It is my heart's desire for every reader of this book to be compelled to start on a spiritual journey, but please do not rush headlong into a situation you will forever regret.

Suicide

It is my belief that the greatest spiritual sin we can commit is to take another's life. The second greatest sin we can commit is to take our own life.

If during the course of your life in this physical realm, you ever, even for a moment, contemplate taking your own life, please seek help. Cry out; seek professional help;

talk to family, friends, loved ones, or anyone for that matter. Get the aid you need to have the courage and strength to live the life God meant for you to live. Please, never let events or other people drive you to the brink of destroying yourself. God loves all of his children, and he created you to live a life of joy, not despair.

I honestly say to you that if you have the strength and courage to face the events that have brought you to this point in your life, you will triumph over the greatest and darkest challenge this life can throw at you. From this point on, you will be able to live your life knowing that you have looked death in the face and beaten it. No one will ever perform a more courageous act during their lifetime. It will give you the strength to face all future obstacles with a new confidence. God will smile at your strength and you will, too.

Loneliness

God made us beings of community and beings of socialization. He made us to be compassionate, caring and sharing. If you are feeling lonely or alone, do what may seem like the hardest thing to do: Seek out other people. We were made to be in the company of others. When we shut others out of our lives, we are in essence shutting God out also.

There are many ways to get involved with other people to beat the feeling of loneliness. Join a professional organization; volunteer at a hospital, food shelter or social services agency; take a class; join a bowling league or a garden club; do whatever it takes to fall in love with living life.

What I am about to say may raise a few eyebrows, but I believe the reason that God created us is because he was lonely. He looked out on the beauty and the vastness of his creation and he had no one to share it with. So he created us to share with him the endless beauty and mysteries of his universe. I believe that God did not want to be alone, and that he does not want us to be alone.

Ghosts

Do I believe that ghosts really exist? Yes, I do. Not the chain-rattling, bed-sheet-covered spirits usually associated with *Casper* and his friends, but real, spiritual entities. There are a great many things that we do not understand about realms, dimensions and the spiritual world. I believe that sometimes, when someone is not ready to cross over, when someone becomes more attached to the physical world than to the spiritual world, they get confused and stay here. I also believe that they will not be here forever; eventually a being from the spiritual realm will take them where they belong. I also honestly believe that there are reputable psychics in the physical world who can help them find their way.

Heaven

A lot has been written about heaven over the centuries. Most depict heaven as a physical place where we spend eternity glorifying God. Some have described heaven as being made up of different realms. I have come to believe that heaven is not a physical place, but a spiritual place that does indeed consist of various realms. When a spirit leaves a physical body, it transcends to the spiritual realms, and which realm it goes to depends upon the life it has just left and the review of that life.

We all have spiritual lessons to learn as well as human and emotional lessons to learn. We have actions to account for and penance to pay. I am convinced that God does not want us to spend eternity on bended knee, glorifying him. I maintain that God has no ego, and that he is not a God who wants to spend eternity hearing endless praise from endless multitudes. There will be a place for each of us and a job to do. There will be spiritual work that needs to be done throughout eternity and God wants us to roll up our sleeves and get to work. He wants us to continuously help each other for all of eternity. Heaven to me is Endless Time, Endless Universe and Endless Knowledge gained through never-ending experiences. Our spiritual growth never ends, and the glowing bath of God's love resonates throughout the very core of our soul.

Hell

Like heaven, hell is not a physical place. I believe that God did not create hell; we humans created hell by our evil actions and evil intentions. And yes, I also believe that there are various realms of hell. Not like the nine levels of hell as described in Dante's *Inferno*, but spiritual realms of reflection, penance and growth. We were not cast into hell by God; we were placed there ourselves, by our own actions and our own conduct.

There are spiritual lessons to be learned from hell just as there are spiritual lessons to be learned from heaven. We have transgressions to atone for and debts owed to other souls to account for. Who decides who goes to heaven and who goes to hell? We do, each and every day, in the decisions we make, by our conduct, and especially by our actions toward other people and toward God's natural world. We control our soul's destiny by how we live our life here on Earth.

Free will was most definitely a gift of awesome responsibility and self-control. The good news is that hell is not eternal, and we will make our way out of returning to hell by living subsequent lives of compassion, love and understanding.

Angels and Demons

Do demonic forces exist? Yes, I believe they do. When God created man, he knew that as beings with free will, we would at times be our own worst enemies. If God is an all-knowing god, and I believe he is, he would have known that a fallen angel would become Satan; and being a merciful, compassionate and loving god, as I believe he is, he would not knowingly create such evil.

God did not put evil into the world, but I think he knew that the collective impurities of man would create evil. I believe that supernatural evil beings do exist and they feed off of the evil of man. Our evil thoughts, deeds and desires feed these creatures of darkness. The good news is, when we stop feeding them, they will cease to exist.

I also believe that God created his legions of angels to protect us from ourselves—sort of spiritual baby sitters, if you will. It is my conclusion that evil and darkness cannot exist in God's presence, or in God's universe, except through man. That is why we spend so many lifetimes purifying ourselves before we can be in God's presence.

God's angels are here to help us. The goal is to stay spiritually connected to God, to always show love and compassion and empathy toward your fellow man. Evil is drawn to darkness, and evil will have no place in your world if you are a being of light.

Questions of Atheism

"Give a man a fish, and you will feed him for a day; give him a religion, and he'll starve to death while praying for a fish."
—Anonymous, from The Atheist's Bible

There are some questions that are overwhelming and unanswerable. If we contemplate them, we soon learn that they are beyond our comprehension and understanding. Where did God come from? Who created God or how could God create himself? What was here before

God? There are endless questions concerning the very foundation of creation and the creator. Questions like these make it easy for someone to throw their hands up in utter frustration and say, "It is much easier to choose not to believe."

We cannot possibly know the answers to these questions in our human lives and may still not know the answers in our spiritual lives. Possibly only God knows the answers to all questions and has complete and infinite knowledge.

Do you know how the atmosphere was formed or why there is air? Scientifically we can find the answers or theories behind these questions, but that is not the point. For most of us, we do not know. All we know is that air fills our lungs and we live. This is the same approach we have to take toward the questions of how and why God came to be. We do not know how or why; we are just thankful that it is.

I think some atheists are atheists because of the complexity of trying to understand it all. It is much easier to simply not believe anything. Some people do not understand tragedy or pain, and they feel as though God has abandoned them or does not exist. I believe God knows something we don't. We do not understand what God understands. God knows that once we cross over to the spiritual realm, everything will be okay. We will be comforted, loved and healed by spiritual loved ones and friends.

I assume atheists who read this will laugh and call me a fool, much as C.S. Lewis would call me a fool for my description of Jesus as a teacher who came back to the physical realm out of compassion for mankind. I do not want to argue the merits of believing or not believing in God. For me, it is not by blind faith that I believe, but from research and contemplation of facts, events and evidence that I believe we are eternal beings created by God. I am awed by witnessing the birth of a baby or the countless other miracles that occur daily in our lives. If you have doubts about the existence of God, do you have an answer as to who created the universe and us? Do you think something so intricate just merely happened? Looking at scientific evidence and theories of creation, I came to the conclusion that the universe and humans are not the results of an accident, but are created by design. An oft-quoted phrase sums it up: "For the believer there is no question; for the non-believer there is no answer."

Faith

Faith is belief in something when there is no proof or reason to support that belief. Sometimes faith is described with terms like "blind faith" or "leap of faith." Isn't that exactly what we do when we fall in love or get married or have children?

I believe that faith also includes an unwavering allegiance, a conviction that you are correct in your beliefs. It is my hope that you never lose your faith in God, never lose the belief that you are eternal and never lose hope in knowing that God loves you. I believe that almost every religion on the planet can agree to that.

We should look for ways that unify us, not ways that separate us. Never, ever let anything or anyone shake your unmistakable faith in yourself and your essence as a truly remarkable spiritual being. You were chosen by God to be with him. Keep the faith each and every day!

CHAPTER 14

WHISPERING TO GOD

14

"Let us be silent that we may hear the whisper of God."
—Ralph Waldo Emerson

Over the course of our earthly lives, we are constantly whispering to God and he to us. With all of the distractions that surround us, his voice, and our thoughts, are barely audible and easily swept away. There are issues that require our undivided attention, and finding our spirituality is one of them.

Bold Statement

What I am about to say is a statement that could cause quite an uproar, but I believe it to be true. Our life is not about God. It is about us.

That may sound like a contradiction to what this book has been about—finding God. Yet, it is my point that in the search for God, we find ourselves. It is my belief that God wants that for us. He created us and gave us life. I do not believe that he would do that and want us to be miserable or without purpose. By focusing on our spiritual nature, the process inevitably leads us to who we really are. When a person fine-tunes their focus on their spirituality, they find peace with themselves, and their relationships with all those around them improve and are more fully appreciated.

Have you ever thought about what type of husband, wife, father, mother, son, daughter or friend you are? When a person starts to seek God and to nurture the spiritual side of life, I maintain that they realize what is truly important: the other living people and things in their life. Once we start looking for God, we find so much more.

During the course of our lives, our internal scars can be magnified and emotional turmoil may be brought to the surface. Our search forces us to face issues about ourselves in a sort of cleansing fashion. This is the way that God designed it. We cannot find him until we find ourselves first. We discover that we must first put ourselves on the right path, and heal our internal psychological and emotional wounds. Facing our faults is part of spiritual growth.

There Is a Path for Everyone

There are some people who may not want to look for God because they are either ashamed of themselves or like their lifestyle without God in it. For those who do not want to look for God because they are ashamed, for whatever reason, that is exactly when they should look for him. He wants to help wash away the shame and cleanse the soul. I believe God is a healing, loving god who does not want to see his children suffer.

If you do not want to search for God or your own spirituality because you like your life without thinking about those things, I believe that karma will take you for a ride you will not enjoy. You cannot carry anything with you from this life except your actions, your deeds and your indifferences.

Purpose of Life

We view our life's mission to be more mysterious than it really is. In Chapter 2, you were asked about your purpose in life. My answer: Our purpose is to live the life God intended us to live. What does that mean? For me, that means to be happy with who I am and to not try to be someone I am not. For me, it means to grow both humanly and spiritually; to seek inner peace and spiritual maturity; to seek my own path to God; and to become a true member of God's family.

How can you determine the life that God intended you to live? Seek your own path to God and I believe it will be revealed to you.

In the beginning of this book, I stated that the complex boils down to a few simple truths. My truths:

Your life matters, however ordinary or extraordinary. It is the journey of your soul and it absolutely matters.

God is real.

We are all eternal.

Our journeys and experiences are eternal. I have learned to focus on the beauty, the life lesson, the wonder, the love and the peace that is always around me. When we set our minds on living life to the fullest, I believe that we can enjoy all that God has given us, including the challenges. Life is about us, how God wants us to enjoy and learn and grow. God is always there, listening for our whispers. I feel that we do not reach God on bended knee, but through purity of heart. He will give us as much time and as many lives as we need.

Epitaph

I have drafted something of an epitaph, but I do not want it on my tombstone. That grave is just a container for a body that will no longer contain my soul. I believe death is the gateway to the spiritual realm and then to the next physical life. If I could speak at my own funeral regarding the end of this life and my ultimate dwelling with God, I would say:

"My life was a common life, but a good life. My death will be a common death, but a good death. No burial of kings for me; just a child of God, on to the next great adventure. I will continue to be a whisper in God's ear and he in mine, until I am worthy to be in his presence. What a truly glorious day that will be. I will be embraced within his loving cloak of spirituality and I will say, 'Father, I have made the journey laid before me from the foundations of creation, I have come home, and I am eternally grateful to you for creating me.'"

CHAPTER 15
YOUR JOURNEY AWAITS

15

"A man has made at least a start on discovering the meaning of human life when he plants shade trees under which he knows full well he will never sit"
—D. Elton Trueblood

Our journey toward God is the adventure of the centuries, and each of us has our own individual adventure. Along the way, our aches, pains, emotional bruises and heartaches of the physical realm will pale in comparison to the finish line waiting for us in the spiritual realm.

This entire book has been written with the thought of you, the reader, embarking on your own spiritual journey of discovery. Do not be intimidated; you do not need to learn everything the first day or the first year or the first decade, or even the first lifetime. Take your time and enjoy the journey. There is no need to rush through it; it is never-ending.

There is an ancient Chinese saying: "If happiness is your destination, you need not be in a hurry." Don't rush through your life with your eyes on the horizon and miss what is at your feet. I cannot stress this enough: We must live in the here and now. Live and experience each moment, each minute, hour and day.

Our path leads us to God, but it is the journey that is important. The rewards will not be monetary or materialistic; they will be more subtle and also more satisfying than that. They will be the understanding of who you are, an opening of your eyes and a glimpse of the spiritual world around you. They will be the rewards that truly count in this life and in lives to come, rewards that nurture your soul and give you courage and inner peace.

African tribesmen have a saying: "If you want to go fast, go alone; if you want to go far, go with others!" In our lives, we are doing both. We have our own personal path to God, but we do not travel that path at the expense of others. We are all kindred souls, all striving to follow our own individual paths, yet we must be mindful of others who interact with us during our journey.

Your intuition is your guide in this lifetime. It is more than just a feeling; it is the spiritual compass to guide you on your life's path and lesson plan. Intuition is an implanted instructional guideline for your life.

Listen and tune in to your intuition; let it be your guide and your compass. Just as you may study and work at learning the lessons of history, geography, math, science, etc., you must also work at and learn the spiritual aspects of your life—how to tune into intuition, meditation, spiritual healing, universal love, compassion, forgiveness, etc. Intuition is the tingling you feel in your brain; it is your spiritual alarm clock.

Don't be afraid to seek the truth wherever it might be. Do not close your mind to all possibilities and do not limit yourself. For example, if you don't believe that ghosts exist, that is understandable, but don't close your mind to the prospect. Read about it, research it and in the end, you can make an educated decision. If you come to the same conclusion that ghosts do not exist, at least now you will make this affirmation from a position of knowledge, a position that backs your belief with facts and evidence.

All I want is for you to be the best spiritual person you can be. If that concept exists in your organized religion, regardless of the faith or denomination, that is wonderful. I want you to live the life God wanted you to live, and I want you to enjoy your life and to be excited by the possibilities and endless glory of God's creation.

Be the person God meant you to be. Find out who you are, find out who God is, and discover your relationship with each other.

Your journey awaits.

SUGGESTED READING

The books listed represent many varied points of view from many varied authors and religions. I agree with some of the ideas, theologies, concepts or views of these authors, and some I do not. However, since my book has been written in an effort to get you, the reader, started on your own spiritual journey, the books listed here represent a small part of my research. They are a well-rounded base from which to start your own journey.

Also, I have suggested additional books by some authors by merely stating, "Plus many others." I do not want to have an outrageously long list nor do I want to sway your opinion. If you like the message or topic from a particular author, read everything that they have written. I did! I can honestly say that some of the names on this list include my greatest heroes with regard to influencing my personal spiritual journey and keeping me excited and hungry in finding my path to spirituality.

I have read literally hundreds of books on religion and spirituality over the past fifteen years. It has been and continues to be the most spiritually exciting thing that I have done with my life. The truly great thing is that you do not have to be wealthy to start on your own journey of discovery. Just go to your local library, pick up a library card and your journey has begun! Do it today. Every soul needs nurturing, and every body and spirit need a lift. Don't go through life being only a small portion of what you were truly meant to be. Be the complete package, body and soul! You will wake up each and every day, and know what a wondrous gift this life really is.

I promise you, your life will make a new and exciting change, and you will never be the same!

My list, in alphabetical order:

Mitch Albom, *Tuesdays With Morrie*

Da Avabhasa (The Bright), and other books published under Adi Da Samraj, such as *Easy Death* and *The Knee of Listening*

Dr. Janis Amatuzio, M.D., *Forever Ours*

Regarding Buddhism—there have been so many excellent books written, I could not possibly list them all

Francis S. Collins, *The Language of God*

Deepak Chopra, *How to Know God,* plus many others

Dr. Wayne Dyer, *Your Sacred Self,* plus many others

John Edward, *After Life,* plus many others

His Holiness, the Dalai Lama, *My Land and My People*, plus many others

Elaine Pagels, *The Gnostic Gospels*

His Holiness, Pope John Paul II, *Crossing The Threshold of Hope,* plus many others

Bishop Anthony M. Pilla, Bishop of Cleveland, *Live On In My Love*

James Van Praagh, *Heaven and Earth,* plus many others

Elisabeth Kubler Ross, M.D., *On Death and Dying,* plus many others

Dr. Ian Stevenson, M.D., *Twenty Cases Suggestive of Reincarnation*, plus many others

Dr. Brian L. Weiss, M.D., *Many Lives, Many Masters,* plus many others

MY PSALM

Like everyone going through the challenges of everyday life, there were times when I would become quite anxious or stressed by the events of the day. On one particular day, during meditation late in the evening, I could not quiet my mind. The day's events kept replaying over and over, and I was still very much in an agitated state. Finally in utter defeat, I asked for help to calm my restless spirit, and what came to me were these words. I wrote the words down, and said the prayer a few times. My agitation went away. Afterwards I felt peaceful and uplifted.

After many years as a Christian, I am sure that there is nothing new in my psalm. However, it represents my own prayer, in my own words, and I honestly say it each and every day at least twice. It gives me spiritual focus, and I do get comfort just from saying the words. The reality is that we often ignore our spiritual side and it is the most important aspect of who we are, though many people do not realize it. Saying my prayer every day helps me understand my existence and I want you to be helped, too.

This particular prayer was me asking for help and being truly thankful for the life I have, with all of its trials and challenges. I came to appreciate how truly blessed my life was, even though things did not always go the way I wanted or hoped for. How could I possibly be upset when I realized that I was created by God, to be with him for the long haul, until the end of time? Each day is a gift, and never again will I let the day's events steal the day away from me.

This was my own private prayer to God. It was never intended to be published. It was me talking to God and thanking him for choosing me. Now, I realize that maybe it can help others also. If you decide to try this yourself, don't just lip sync the words; say them with feeling and honestly mean them. Of course, you can draft a prayer of your own. Take some time every day to talk to God. If you don't feel any different after starting this regime, I will be very surprised.

I wish for you a journey of discovery, of profound joy and of deep and lasting peace. Thank you for reading.

—Tom

TOM ACIERNO

My Psalm

GOD, Almighty Father,
Please comfort my restless spirit,
Let my soul be at peace.

Heal me with your holy embrace,
Comfort me in your quiet stillness,
And forgive me my weaknesses.

I thank you for this day,
In all of its trials and joys.
And I thank you for what
Each new day brings.

I am grateful for those who
Spiritually surround and support me.
Thank you, Father, for bestowing them onto me,
And I thank them for their nurturing spirit.

Thank you for creating me.
Thank you for the most blessed gift of
My family, friends and loved ones.

Thank you, Father, for your love, and
Everything you have done for me.
I pray for the day I can
Thank you in a heart born of spirit.